Shakespeare Then & Again
THE TRAGEDY OF MACBETH

Sanghamitra Dasgupta

INDIA • SINGAPORE • MALAYSIA

ISBN 979-8-89133-942-2

Contents

Acknowledgements

As in my first book, I have gone back to my friend Ms. Susmita Bhattacharya for the cover design. I express my heartfelt gratitude for her support in giving me a cover so evocative of the "darkness" that the play Macbeth embodies.

I would also like to mention my colleague at NDLI, Ms. Manami Mukherjee, who has given me both mental and physical support. She has painstakingly typed part of the manuscript and extended her helping hand whenever I needed. Without her help, I would not have been able to meet the deadline. Thank you, Manami.

Another colleague who helped me with the images in the book is Mr. Bibhash Roy. I am grateful to him too.

This is an academic book for students and so I have used pictures from the internet. In case, I have inadvertently infringed any copyright rules, I would like to be informed at the earliest for rectification.

Foreword

The Tragedy of Macbeth by William *Shakespeare* is the third in the series *Shakespeare: Then and Again,* the first two being *The Merchant of Venice* and *The Tempest.* This book has been designed keeping in mind the principles enumerated in NEP 2020 that calls for a multidisciplinary and inclusive approach to education. The book therefore has sections on history to give students an understanding of the times when the events occurred and uses techniques of mind mapping and pictorial representation to promote inclusiveness.

The NEP 2020 also envisages a holistic education. It stresses on promotion of critical thinking and practical application abilities of the students as well as inculcation of value questions. All the questions and answers referring to the actual Shakespearean text of the play have been framed in accordance with these principles.

The book is therefore divided into four sections. The first section *Blow the Bagpipe and the Bugle* gives the historical background of Scotland with regard to the play. The second *Under the Microscope* deals with details of the play itself in sub-divisions dealing with character analyses, themes, MCQs, SAQs and Essay-type questions and answers. The third section *Towards the Finishing Line* encourages Higher Order Thinking among students while the fourth *To Read or Not to Read* has essays by the author reflecting on Macbeth, its increased relevance in the dystopian world and more.

1
Blow the Bagpipe and the Bugle

GLIMPSES OF ANCIENT SCOTTISH HISTORY

The novels of Sir Walter Scott and the numerous Scottish ballads portray a Scotland that, though torn by feuds and clan warfare, is essentially a land of romance and poetry with its misty Highlands and fertile Lowlands. Today it is more popular for its whiskey, bagpipes and kilts or tartans as well as of course, the Loch Ness monster. Modern Scotland has a fascinating and complex history with the pre-historic tribes of the Caledonians, Picts and the Scots, the Vikings and Roman generals all fighting fierce battles to gain control over this part of the British Isles.

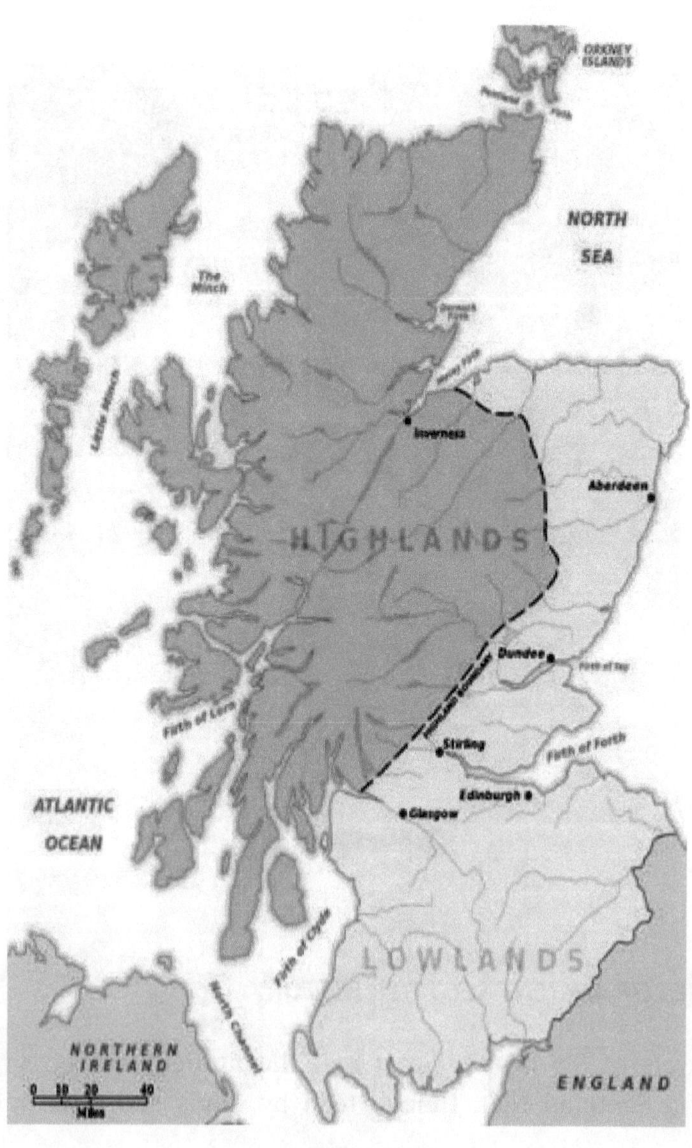

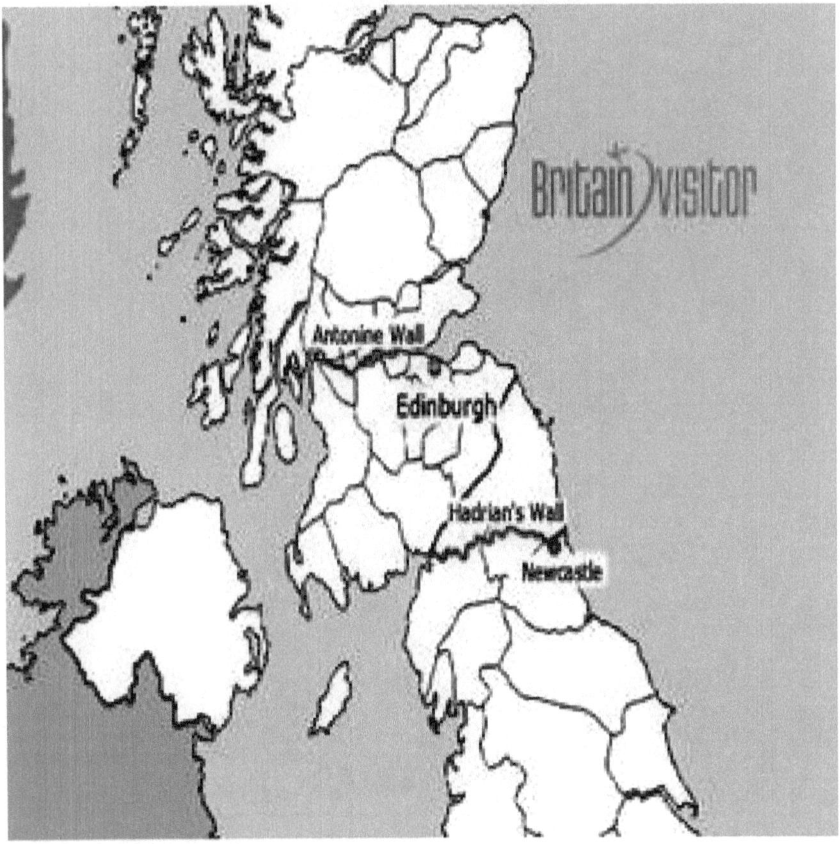

Britain visitor
Antonine Wall
Edinburgh
Hadrian's Wall
Newcastle

Prehistoric Scottish ruins discovered at Orkney give an idea of the lives of the nomadic hunter-gatherers as well as the first farmers. The country's recorded history starts in 43 CE with the arrival of the Romans who, despite Julius Caesar and later Emperor Hadrian, could not get a strong foothold in the land and retreated from what was then known as Caledonia.

Two ruins – the Hadrian Wall (122 CE) and the Antoine Wall (142 CE) – remain mute witnesses of history.

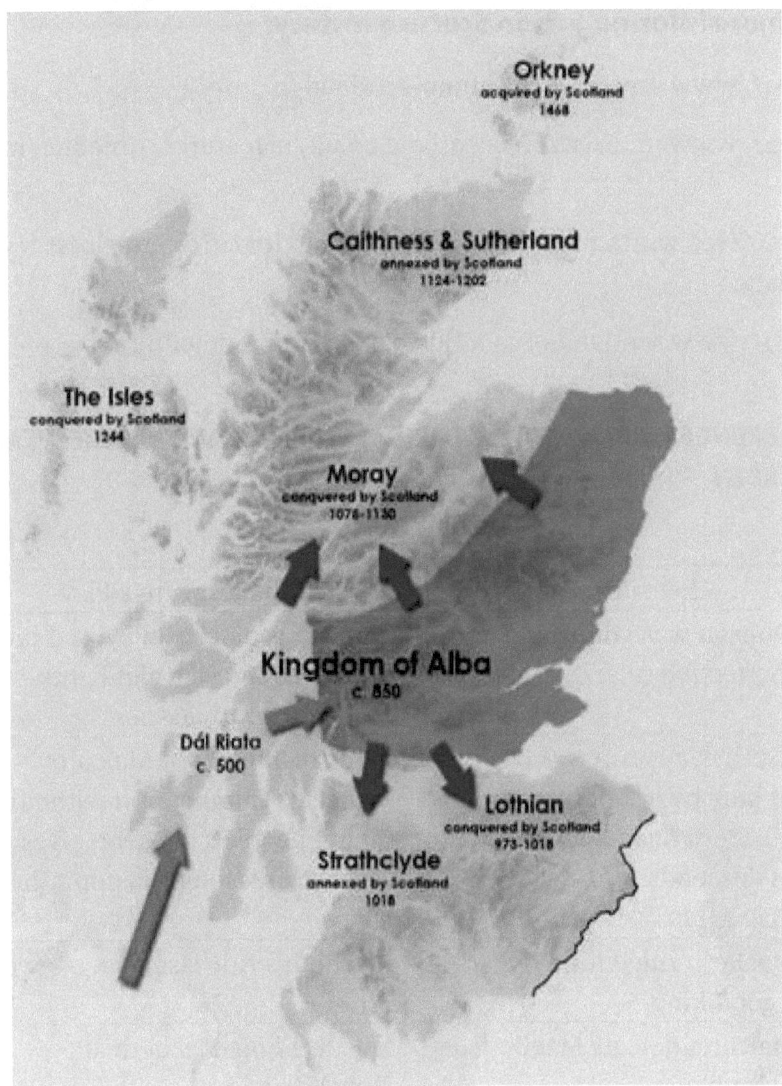

In 1100 CE, the tribal way of life was replaced by a feudal society. William I of Alba, compelled to sign the Treaty of Falaise with England's Henry II in 1174 BCE, ushered in an era of relative peace and the land was turned over more to agriculture. It flourished in the reigns of succeeding kings, Alexander II and Alexander III; monasteries and abbeys grew in number as trade with the Continent had a positive impact on the economy.

The kingdom of Alba became Scotland *circa* 1286 CE.

For more information on Scottish history:

https://www.scotland.org/about-scotland/history

https://www.undiscoveredscotland.co.uk/usfeatures/timeline/index.html

https://www.nts.org.uk/learning/adult-learning/the-history-of-scotland

https://www.scotland.org.uk/history/heritage-timeline

DIFFERENCES BETWEEN HISTORICAL EVENTS AND SHAKESPEARE'S MACBETH

Historical Fact	Shakespeare's Play
1. Duncan was young and an ineffective ruler.	Duncan is elderly, wise and much loved; his murder highlights Macbeth's ruthlessness
2. Scottish custom was election of king by the people; MacBeth had legitimate claim as descendant of Kenneth Mac Alpin	Duncan appointed Malcolm as Prince of Cumberland without taking people's consent; gives Macbeth reason to commit the crime
3. MacBeth ruled for 17 years as a good king	Macbeth's rule lasts just one year; tyrant
4. Malcolm defeats MacBeth at Lumphanan	Macduff kills Macbeth at Dunsinane
5. Banquo accomplice in Duncan's murder	Banquo himself murdered; since King James claimed descendance from Banquo through the Stuart line, he couldn't be portrayed as the king's murderer

SNIPPETS :

- Action of the play takes place over nine days while the historical events occurred over a period of eighteen years.

- Macbeth first appeared in the First Folio of 1623. There is no quarto or any other version of it before this.

- There is a first hand account of the play's performance at the Globe on April 20, 1610 by Dr. Simon Forman in his diary entries made in 1610 and 1611.

Shakespeare pays tribute to King James throughout the play – overflow of Biblical imagery reflecting James' great passion for the Scripture that culminated in *King James Version* of the Bible in 1611, his interest in witchcraft as reflected in his book *Daemonologie* woven into *Macbeth*, "two-fold ball and treble sceptres" (IV,i) referring to the globes or royal insignia of James as King of Scotland and England and the three sceptres the three kingdoms of England, Scotland and Ireland.

2

Under the Microscope

<u>Macbeth</u> takes a deep dive into the psyche of a man who travels the path from glory to damnation consciously and dies heroically with spirit unbowed. It deals with the complexities of a man's character that arise from the tussle between his conscience and his yearning. It is a dark and bloody play filled with murder and mayhem, the rare bursts of light only deepening the darkness. The clash of illusion and reality, innocence and guilt, the natural and the unnatural, order and disorder all make for a modern psychological thriller and one waits with bated breath for the finish. Yet it is also a 'morality' play for it conveys the message that the use of evil means do not make for happy endings. However one looks at it, <u>Macbeth</u> is undoubtedly one of Shakespeare's finest tragedies.

CHARACTERS

1. **Macbeth:** Perhaps no character of Shakespeare's is as complex as Macbeth. Is he a villain or a tragic hero? Is he an anti-hero? Is he "Bellona's bridegroom" or one "afeard/To be the same in thine own act and valour"? Is he a ruthless and bloody butcher of children or a puppet in the hands of fate? He is, in fact, all of the above and more. He is a murderer at the mercy of his conscience that constantly pricks him till he bleeds as much as his victims. And this, despite the complete transformation from a noble warrior to ambition's slave, is what makes him a tragic hero despite his villainy.

    Macbeth enters with the words "So foul and fair a day I have not seen." This juxtaposition of the fair and the foul runs through Macbeth's character as well. In the beginning, we see Macbeth the general who leads from the front, the life and soul of Duncan's army. It is his prowess and leadership that enables Duncan to be victorious over the rebel Macdonwald – "For brave Macbeth – well he deserves that name --/Disdaining fortune, with his brandished steel,/Which smoked with bloody execution...". Such is the fire of loyalty burning in him that even the fresh assault by the King of Norway aided by the traitorous Thane of Cawdor has no effect on his ardour. Ross and Angus' descriptions paint a picture of a Viking or a Nordic god. And yet Macbeth's response to the three Witches have already given us a glimpse of the foul in him. It is implied in Banquo's words "Good Sir, why do you start and seem to fear/ Things that do sound so fair?" Macbeth, too, is aware of his "deep and dark desires" and is apprehensive of them.

And this brings us to the constant turmoil in him. Against his wife's accusations of cowardice and being "too full of the milk of human kindness", he firmly declares "I dare do all that may become a man/ He dares do more is none." And yet he cannot let go of the jewel he yearns for – "the golden round." Despite his misgivings, he finally yields to temptation – not, as sometimes said, because of Lady Macbeth's incitement or the witches' prophecies but because of his own burning desire. He can not ignore his own "Vaulting ambition" and embarks on a path of brutal and horrible massacre.

What saves him from being a heartless villain is that he loses all peace of mind. He has a powerful imagination that makes him hallucinate about daggers dripping with blood, makes him feel that the blood on his hands can never be washed off, instead it will the "multitudinous seas incarnadine", makes him hear cries of "Glamis hath murthered Sleep, and therefore Cawdor/Shall sleep no more, Macbeth shall sleep no more!"

And so Macbeth elevates himself to the position of tragic hero by always acknowledging his failure to rise above his frailties. His soliloquies reveal the inner conflict that becomes his constant companion. The more terrible his actions, the more sensitive his reactions and the more heroic his battle. In the long run, Macbeth is defeated not by Macduff but by his own conscience. After committing the heinous crime of regicide against one who had come to him in "double trust", Macbeth says that with the king gone,

"....renown, and grace, is dead;/The wine of life is drawn, and the mere lees/Is left this vault to brag of." He is talking more of himself than the king. His soliloquies raise him to heroic levels for no villain can mouth such truths through such divine poetry.

Every time he falls to the depths of the damned, he rises to greater heights of heroism.

2. **Lady Macbeth:** Lady Mabeth's character was dismissed as evil by many earlier critics because of her incitement to Macbeth. She has also been labelled as the Fourth Witch of the play. It was perhaps because of the patriarchal societal construct of the times. Yet a close reading of her speeches reveal her to be a woman who wanted to be powerful in her own right. Jacobean society had a strict code for women had choked her potential and rendered her powerless. Shakespeare defies that social construct by characterising Lady Macbeth as a symbol of power and not of weak femininity.

That Lady Macbeth is an equal partner in their marriage is apparent from the letter Macbeth sends her. It reveals that she has been a party to his thoughts and that they have discussed together the matter of succession to the Scottish throne. She is astute in the judgement of her husband's character – "…..what thou wouldst highly,/That thou wouldst holily…" She is ambitious too yet would rather not commit the crime herself. Instead, she wants to propel Macbeth towards it with the "valour of her tongue." She is, therefore, not as strong as she wants to believe. And it is for this very reason that she has to call upon Spirits to "unsex" her, to fill her from top to toe with the "direst cruelty" so that she becomes devoid of pity. Had she been a witch or even just a devil woman, certainly she would not have had to call for such help. For Macbeth, in fact, the very thought of the dire deed had shaken his "single state of man", and Lady Macbeth has to urge "murther'ng ministers" to turn her milk into gall so that not the slightest strain of womanhood remain in her.

However, she fails to wrench out the inherent tenderness in herself and this becomes apparent when she returns from Duncan's chamber without killing him because the king had resembled her father as he slept. Though she is her strong assertive self in the

Banquet Scene, her presence vanishes just afterwards as Macbeth embarks on a whirlwind of action. She is his "dearest chuck" whom he would shelter from the coming storm. Were she a witch or evil, such protection would be completely unnecessary!

Lady Macbeth at first arouses awe because of the force of her initial speeches. Many critics call her cunning because she goads her husband on to the path of damnation. What is forgotten is that Macbeth's ambition had already made him contemplate that path. Had he thought it completely wrong, he had the strength of character not to give in to her persuasions. Therefore, instead of blame, she evokes admiration for the support she gives her husband whenever his confidence becomes shaky.

The final image of Lady Macbeth on stage is that of a woman who has lost the battle between her desires and her conscience. From that formidable woman calling on supernatural powers to make her 'unnatural' by taking away her gender, she is reduced to a shadow of her former self, desperately wanting but failing to remove the imaginary stink of blood from her hands "...all the/ perfumes of Arabia will not sweeten this little hand" , a woman slowly losing her mind "To bed, to bed: there's knocking at the gate". Her words "What's done cannot be undone" sum up her tragedy and may serve as a fitting epitaph.

3. **Banquo:** Shakespeare has made Banquo's character a foil to Macbeth to highlight the forces of evil in Macbeth and what happens to one who commits regicide; as an astute businessman, Shakespeare realised that it would also please King James who claimed to be a descendant of Banquo. We find Banquo endowed with all the virtues like bravery, modesty, lack of envy etc.

   Banquo is equal to Macbeth in courage on the battlefield. The bleeding sergeant describes them as "cannons overcharg'd with double cracks" and Duncan himself refers to them as "Our Captains." However, he is shown as superior to Macbeth as a human being. He shows no envy when Duncan goes overboard in praising Macbeth and is almost addressed as an afterthought. His modesty becomes apparent when he makes the self-effacing reply "There if I grow,/

The harvest is your own...." to his sovereign liege. In fact, Macbeth himself voices this difference between them as he contemplates Banquo's murder -- "....'tis much he dares,/And to that dauntless temper of his mind/He hath wisdom that doth guide his valour/ To act in safety." And Banquo's wisdom keeps him anchored to the right path.

Banquo is an acutely perceptive man. Something that is remarkable in Banquo is his knowledge of Macbeth's nature. Right from the beginning he keeps warning Macbeth not to give in to his imaginings. He tells Macbeth that "the instruments of darkness" betray people into doing wrong by winning their trust with "honest trifles." He becomes suspicious of Macbeth when Macbeth invites him to declare his loyalty and promises rewards. Without any hesitation, Banquo asserts that he cannot and will not do anything that will his stain his honour or question his allegiance to King Duncan. This unequivocal and fearless rebuff is admirable, especially since he is already plagued by doubts about Macbeth and the prophecies that have kept him awake too. It is his strong moral sense that makes him finally reject the promptings of his dreams and pray for god's grace.

And yet, something stops him from sharing his suspicions with others, especially Malcolm, Donalbain and Macduff. It is here that we find Banquo's characterisation rather incomplete. Why does he not confront Macbeth in private? This remains open to debate. Perhaps Shakespeare did not want to give king and patron King James I even the slightest reason for dislike. However, his dramatic sensibilities did not allow him to make Banquo a bland ideal of the virtuous hero as the contrast to the villain Macbeth's thrilling complexity. That would certainly have ruined the effect of the play. So perhaps Shakespeare preferred to leave us wondering and draw our own conclusions. Banquo remains an enigmatic character, especially in relation to both Macbeth and Macduff.

4. **Macduff:** Just as Banquo is a foil to Macbeth, Macduff is a foil to Banquo. If anyone can claim to be the 'hero' of the play, it is Macduff for he has all the virtues of a leader and a patriot. He is alert to

situations, quick to question whatever seems suspicious, selfless and empathetic. Banquo, despite all the virtues in him, does not quite measure up to Macduff's integrity of character.

Macduff's love for his liege is expressed in his description of Duncan's murder: "O horror! Horror! Horror!/ Tongue nor heart cannot conceive, nor name thee..." There is no doubt about the sincerity of his emotional reaction. All his senses rise up against such a foul deed and Macbeth's killing of the only witnesses to the murder, raises his suspicions and he is quick to ask "Wherefore did you so?" Macbeth's answer fails to satisfy him and he expresses his fears to Lenox "Lest our old robes sit easier than our new."

Macduff wastes no time in declaring his enmity towards Macbeth once he is convinced of Macbeth's treachery. He refuses to attend the royal banquet called by Macbeth after he has been crowned thus making it clear to one and all that he would oppose Macbeth's succession tooth and nail. To this end, he rushes off to England without a second thought to offer his services to Malcom, whom Duncan had crowned Prince of Cumberland before his death. His patriotism is unquestionable for he pays a high price for it – he loses his wife and sons to Macbeth's sword. Not that he loved them less but that he loved Scotland, now his "down-fallen birthdom", more.

Macduff as shown in the play is held in high esteem by his countrymen as "the good Macduff" and it is his nobility and superior morality that enrages Macbeth. He makes Macbeth realise what he should have been but is not. And so Shakespeare makes Macduff the instrument of divine justice in the play. A man of few words, he allows his actions to speak for him. His killing of Macbeth signals a restoration of order in Scotland.

THEMES AND MOTIFS

i. <u>Violence:</u> The play is an exploration of the nature of violence. One is considered a brave patriot when fighting for the state but is labelled a rebel when using violence against the state. We have always seen that violence when used by authority or state is condoned while violence used against them is condemned. So long as the defence forces and the police follow the government's orders, they are bravely doing their duty; as soon as they disobey, perhaps prompted by conscience, they are said to have run rogue. Throughout the play, we see this tussle between condoned and condemned violence.

ii. <u>Equivocation:</u> A very important theme in *Macbeth* is that of equivocation. The Witches' greetings to Macbeth are the first examples of half-truths or equivocations. The Porter Scene makes a direct reference to equivocation through the entry of the equivocator. Again, the utterances of the first two apparitions are equivocations for they give Macbeth a false sense of security and propel him to his tragic death. Their words "none of woman born" can vanquish him and that he will remain undefeated till "Birnam Wood to high Dunsinane hill/Shall come against him" are perfect to soothe his fears and ensnare him into a deluded complacency.

iii. <u>Ambition:</u> Macbeth's tragic flaw is his "vaulting ambition" and the word "vaulting" is the key word, conveying an ambition that is boundless and intemperate. Macbeth's ambition is further stoked by the witches' prophecies and his wife's desire. Had he kept his own counsel in the matter, he probably would not have overstepped his boundaries. But then the play would not have had the lofty appeal of a Shakespearean tragedy. The sub-text of the play therefore conveys that so long as one does not become the slave of ambition, ambition cannot and should not to be condemned as a vice.

iv. <u>Destiny (Fate) and Character (Free Will):</u> The tragedy of *Macbeth* is gripping for the very reason that it is difficult to decide which plays the pivotal role – Macbeth's destiny or his character. In the beginning, with the quick fulfilment of the witches' first two prophecies, it seems Macbeth is destined to be king. He says as much to himself "If chance will have me king, why, chance may crown me,/Without my stir." But Macbeth's impatience to attain his destiny is a trait in his character as is his greed for power. The play makes a convincing argument that one's character decides one's destiny; the two are not in opposition but have a symbiotic relationship.

i. <u>Appearance vs. Reality:</u> The play starts with the witches' incantation "Fair is foul and foul is fair" which conveys the difficulty in distinguishing the false (appearance) from the true (reality).

"False face must hide what the false heart doth know" says Macbeth when he has decided to murder Duncan. The motif of what appears to be true not being true in reality runs through the play. The castle of Inverness "hath a pleasant seat" yet lurking within is danger and death. Macbeth must "look like a flower" but "be the serpent under it." Even nearer the end of the play, Malcolm portrays himself as a fiend worse than Macbeth before he confesses to the portrait being false – he appears to be what he is not.

A CLOSE EXAMINATION OF THE PLAY

Act I, Sc i

i. **Multiple Choice Questions**

1. **I took a by-lane to avoid the _____________ of traffic on the main road. Fill in the blank with the word that you have in the scene.**

    a. battle

    b. thunder

    c. congestion

    d. hurly-burly

2. **Which of the following means the same as "When the battle's lost and won"?**

    a. One side wins and the other side loses

    b. Both sides win and lose

    c. One thinks that victory and defeat are the same

    d. Both sides suffer equally

3. **What is the effect of the atmosphere in this scene?**

    a. One feels wary of doing the wrong thing

    b. One has goosebumps

    c. One feels a superstitious fear

    d. One's hackles rise

4. **Graymalkin and Paddock are mentioned in the scene because ___________________. Choose the right option to complete the sentence.**

    a. they lend authenticity to the witches

    b. they decrease the eeriness of the scene

    c. their presence heightens tension

    d. their calls increase the wildness of the heath

5. **"Fair is foul, and foul is fair" – What is the importance of this line in the play?**

    a. presents a change of opinions

    b. portrays the reversal of values

    c. creates a supernatural fear

    d. catches one's imagination

ii. Reference to context

Witch: That will be ere the set of sun.

Witch: Where the place?

Witch: Upon the heath.

i. *Why does Shakespeare open the play with the witches?*

Ans.: <u>Macbeth</u> is a Jacobean play written when King James was the patron of Shakespeare's theatre company, *The King's Men*. James was very interested in witches and witchcraft, having written the treatise *Demonologie* on them and Shakespeare was careful to please his sovereign and royal patron. Shakespeare also wanted to attract the attention of his audience who, like their king, was fascinated and repelled simultaneously by such creatures. Finally, the witches are essential to Shakespeare's exploration of the conflict between good and evil and the establishment of the 'dark' atmosphere of the play.

ii. *What does "That" refer to here?*

Ans. "That" here refers to the battle raging at the time between the loyal generals of Duncan, Macbeth and Banquo, and the rebels led by Macdonwald. As we come to know in the very next scene, it was a fierce battle with Fortune favouring the rebels till Macbeth killed Macdonwald by a brutal stroke from the latter's "nave to the chaps".

iii. *Why did the witches decide to meet Macbeth?*

Ans.: The witches' decision to meet Macbeth is an example of Shakespeare's dramatic skill. He had to make the witches announce the titles awaiting Macbeth in order to foreshadow the underlying forces controlling the action of the play as well as the psychological agony of his protagonist. Taken by his audience as representations of evil according to the Renaissance belief, they must meet Macbeth to prompt him to go against his conscience and tread the path to damnation.

iv. *What is the significance of the meeting place?*

Ans.: The meeting place is a heath which in Old English meant 'wasteland'; its modern usage is more with reference to 'uncultivated tract of land with coarse soil'. Since the setting of the play is in Scotland of the 11th century, 'wasteland' would be closer to fulfilling the dramatist's purpose of portraying the stark barrenness that was waiting for Macbeth in future. So the significance of the meeting place lies in its symbolism.

v. *Explain the significance of "Fair is foul and foul is fair/Hover through the fog and filthy air".*

Ans.: The lines may be said to be the play's leitmotif as they represent the ambiguity of the terms and the constant shift that occurs between them throughout the play. Macbeth, the brave general loyal to his king is "fair" and yet nurses such ambition that involves regicide which is "foul". Duncan himself, "gentle and kind" but not so "fair" because he overrides Scottish tradition in crowning his son the Prince of Cumberland without his thanes' unanimous concurrence. Lady Macbeth, much disdained and derided for her role in needling Macbeth to take the final step is perhaps not as "foul" as she seems initially, for the "bloody deed" drives her finally insane. Torn by rebellion and civil strife, Scotland is enveloped in "fog and filthy air" of disloyalty, fear and suspicion which clears only at the end of the play with the rightful ruler ascending the Scottish throne.

vi. *What effect does this scene have on you?*

Ans.: The scene has a hypnotic effect on me and makes my hair stand on end. The incantatory effect of the single lines spoken in turn by the witches, the noise of thunder and lightning, the witches dressed as women but with beards, Graymalkin's eyes glowing as it pads to the First Witch's side and Paddock's croak lend to the 'dark' or underworld atmosphere that is frightening yet compelling.

Act I, Scene ii

i. **Multiple Choice Questions**

1. **What does Duncan's camping away from the battlefield tell you about him?**

    a.   He was too old to join the battle

    b.   He was afraid of losing his life

    c.   He was not a warrior king

    d.   He was a holy man

2. **Duncan asks "What bloody man is that?" because _______________. Choose the right option to complete the sentence.**

    a.   he was cursing in anger

    b.   the man was bleeding, coming straight from the battlefield

    c.   Duncan felt scared at the sight of the man

    d.   he thought the man was running away from battle

3. **Who strengthened the rebel Macdonwald's forces?**

    a.   Thane of Fife

    b.   King of Cornwall

    c.   Thane of Cawdor

    d.   King of Norway

4.   **What does the clause "but all's too weak" mean in context of the speech?**

    a.   Everything was lost

    b.   The opposition could not stand firm against Macbeth

    c.   Further fighting was useless

    d.   Banquo and Macbeth were not strong enough

5.   **"Like Valour's minion...." – Macbeth is referred to by this epithet because _______________. Choose the correct option to complete the sentence.**

    a.   because he fought so fiercely

    b.   because he behaved so wildly

    c.   because he cut up Macdonwald

    d.   because he was the greatest warrior

6.   **What does Macdonwald's final fate reveal about Macbeth?**

    a.   He was a man possessed by evil

    b.   He was a bloodthirsty man

    c.   He was devoted to Duncan

    d.   He was ruthless in battle

7.   **"O valiant cousin!" – What figure of speech is evident in Duncan's words and why?**

    a.   Apostrophe because he is addressing Macbeth in the latter's absence

    b.   Euphemism because he does not really think that Macbeth has been courageous

    c.   Climax because we finally see Macbeth on stage

    d.   Irony because very soon he will be killed by Macbeth of whom he is so effusive

8. **"So from that spring, whence comfort seems to come/ Discomfort swells." – Which of the following gives the meaning of the lines quoted?**

   a. The spring of life also causes our deaths

   b. Ill-fortune comes from the same quarter that brought good fortune

   c. Comfort and discomfort arise from the sense of fear

   d. Discord always accompanies concord

9. **Which of the following adjectives would you choose for the "Norweyan Lord" mentioned in this scene?**

   a. fearful

   b. appalling

   c. courageous

   d. opportunistic

10. **"Or memorize another Golgotha" – Identify the figure of speech in the given line.**

    a. Personification

    b. Allusion

    c. Metaphor

    d. Pun

11. **The Captain/Sergeant mentions "Golgotha" because _________________. Choose the correct option to complete the sentence.**

    a. Shakespeare wants the audience think of Christ's crucifixion

    b. he wanted to enable his audience to imagine the numbers killed in battle

    c. he wished to show Macdonwald as one who has been wrongly persecuted

    d.   Shakespeare wants to portray Macbeth's resolve to win the battle at all costs

12. **What portrait of Macbeth is painted by the messengers in this scene?**

    a.   a brave general

    b.   a troubled soul

    c.   a disloyal subject

    d.   a warrior king

13. **Which of the following is proof of Macbeth's valour?**

    a.   "Who, like a good and hardy soldier, fought..."

    b.   "As two spent swimmers, that do cling together...."

    c.   "As sparrows eagles, or the hare the lion."

    d.   "....carv'd out his passage...."

14. **What prompted the Norweyan lord to attack Macbeth?**

    a.   He had the support of the Thane of Cawdor

    b.   He thought Macbeth would be too exhausted to fight another battle

    c.   He knew he would get the support of the Scottish people

    d.   He wanted to expand his empire into Scotland

15. **Who does "Bellona" allude to?**

    a.   God of War

    b.   Fortune

    c.   Goddess of War

    d.   Scottish saint

16. **What quality is associated with "Bellona's bridegroom"?**

    a.   ferocity

    b.   courage

    c.   beauty

    d.   greed

17.   **What does the expression "lapp'd in proof" mean?**

    a.   wearing armour to shield oneself against injury

    b.   shrouded in mystery

    c.   protected by a phalanx of soldiers

    d.   enveloped in courage that needs no proof

18.   **"Curbing his lavish spirit..." – What is the meaning of the word 'lavish' here?**

    a.   extravagant

    b.   insolent

    c.   proud

    d.   envious

19.   **How does Norway's king affect the Scottish people?**

    a.   They are petrified by his presence on their lands

    b.   They are happy to assist him

    c.   They are scared of his troops ravaging their land

    d.   They wish to join his army

20.   **Shakespeare's skill as a dramatist becomes apparent in this scene _____________. Choose the right option to complete the sentence.**

    a.   in the way he uses language to convey what he cannot show on stage

    b.   by the way he delineates Macbeth's character as a tormented soul

    c.   through the dialogues between the messengers and Duncan

    d.   in the descriptions of the battles

ii. Reference to Context

1.   Duncan: What bloody man is that? He can report,

The newest state.

Malcolm: This is the Sergeant

Who, like a good and hardy soldier, fought

'Gainst my captivity.

    i.   *Where are the speakers at this point of time? Why does Duncan call the Sergeant "bloody"?*

Ans.: The scene occurs near Forres in Scotland where King Duncan had put up camp as close as possible to the battlefield. The speakers are in Duncan's tent at this point of time.

The Sergeant, as we come to know, has come straight from the battlefield. He is "bloody" because of the blood dripping or oozing from the wounds he has received while fighting.

    ii.   *What "revolt" does Duncan refer to? What does this convey about the political state of Scotland under Duncan?*

Ans.: Duncan refers to the rebellion of Macdonwald, one of the Scottish thanes who had sworn allegiance to Duncan earlier.

Macdonwald's rebellion conveys that at least some of Duncan's people were eager to displace Duncan from the Scottish throne. Scotland was already experiencing political turmoil and perhaps this prompted Duncan to make Malcolm the Prince of Cumberland somewhat hastily. But his desire to send a message of assurance to his people about Scotland's future king had consequences which he had never imagined possible.

    iii.   *How does the Sergeant/Captain describe the battle?*

Ans.: The outcome of the battle initially hung in balance as both Macdonwald and Macbeth fought a fierce battle. Though Fortune at first favoured Macdonwald, Macbeth

"Valour's minion" created havoc in the rebel's ranks before he faced Macdonwald himself. With sheer savagery, he "unseam'd him (Macdonwald) from the nave to th' chops/And fixed his head upon our battlements." There was no time for celebration, however, as Macbeth and Banquo had to immediately engage with the assault of the "Norweyan lord" helped by the traitorous Thane of Cawdor. Both were fighting like cannons loaded with double the charge of the explosives when the Sergeant was forced by his "bloody" wounds to leave the battlefield.

iv.   *What orders does Duncan give at the end of the scene? How are they ironical?*

Ans.: Duncan pronounces the death sentence for the Thane of Cawdor and bestows the title to Macbeth.

Duncan conveys his sorrow that the "gentleman" whom he had trusted implicitly had betrayed him. It is highly ironical that the person who gets the title as a reward for his loyalty will also betray Duncan and in a way far more cruelly than may be imagined. Shakespeare's audience knew that Macbeth would prove a far greater traitor than Cawdor and so the orders foreshadow the tragedy and hence, are ironical.

v.   *What impression do you get of Macbeth from the Sergeant's words? Why does Shakespeare give such a graphic description of the battle?*

Ans.: The Sergeant's words convey the ruthless soldier that Macbeth was. His ferocious savagery is almost inhuman as he neither gives nor asks for any quarter in the battle. His image is one of a fierce Viking warrior drunk with bloodlust and there is a terrifying remorselessness in his actions that portray Macbeth as a pagan god.

In Shakespeare's times, the stage props were minimalistic and the bloody rout could not really be put on stage for the audience. It would create too much horror instead of the admiration and awe that Shakespeare wanted to evoke in his audience. The best way to ensure the effect he wanted was to let the audience imagine the scenes that his words would convey. So he gives this graphic description of the battle – it leaves the impression of Macbeth as an indomitable warrior with unquestioning loyalty for his king. Ultimately, this would make the regicide all the more difficult to believe and accept. An unconscious sympathy is created for Macbeth that will underlie all future response to him.

2. Sergeant: Doubtful it stood;

    As two spent swimmers, that do cling together

    And choke their art. The merciless Macdonwald

    (Worthy to be a rebel, for to that

    The multiplying villainies of nature

    Do swarm upon him) from the western isles

    Of kerns and gallowglasses is supplied;

    And Fortune, ...

    i. *How is the Sergeant introduced to the King? What is his present condition?*

        Ans.: The Sergeant is introduced as the "good and hardy soldier" who had saved Malcolm form being captured by the rebels who were attacking the Scottish King Duncan, Malcolm's father.

        He is called "bloody man" by the King. This conveys that he is bleeding profusely from his wounds.

    ii. *What does the speaker mean by "Doubtful it stood"?*

        Ans.: The Sergeant, in this monologue, describes the fierce battle being fought between Duncan's generals Macbeth and Banquo and the rebel Macdonwald. Both armies under their leaders fought with such ferocity that the fortunes of war swung from one to the other. It seemed they would decimate each other, making it difficult to guess who would triumph over the other. The final outcome of the battle was therefore uncertain.

iii. *Why is Macdonwald called "merciless"? Explain the figure of speech used with reference to him.*

Ans.: Macdonwald is called "merciless" because he is ruthless and displays no sign of relenting even though both he and Macbeth are exhausted. He gives no chance to his opponent to score against him.

A metaphor has been used to describe him. Just as rotten or decaying matter attract nasty insects that swarm over it, Macdonwald attracts all the vices of human nature and they swarm and breed upon him because he is rotten to his core.

iv. *How, according to the Sergeant, does Fortune behave? What is the speaker's reaction to this behaviour?*

Ans.: According to the Sergeant, Fortune behaves like a "rebel's whore". Fortune behaves like a prostitute favouring the rebel Macdonwald instead of King Duncan. Perhaps Fortune was attracted to the rebel because there was something lacking in Duncan as a ruler.

The speaker is outraged at the fickleness of Fortune because she deserts the rightful king of Scotland. He expresses his disgust through these demeaning words.

v. *Do you think the description of the battle echoes the words of the Weird Sisters in the opening scene of the play? Substantiate your answer from the text.*

Ans.: The Weird Sisters had said "When the hurly-burly's done/When the battle's lost and won." The Sergeant seems to echo these very words as he talks about the battle in progress. The clash and clatter of battle as men engage with each other and swords clash with shields, the neighing of the horses trampling over fallen men screaming in pain, all are imaged in the words "hurly-burly". The very fact that the battle seems almost lost till Macbeth wins it by his powerful stroke "from the nave to the chops" that kills Macdonwald echoes "the battle's lost and won."

3. Duncan: Dismay'd not this

Our captains, Macbeth and Banquo?

Sergeant: Yes;

As sparrows eagles, or the hare the lion.

If I say sooth, I must report they were

As cannons overcharg'd with double cracks;

So they

Doubly redoubled strokes upon the foe:

Except they meant to bathe in reeking wounds,

Or memorise another Golgotha,

I cannot tell.

    i.   *What is the context of Duncan's remark?*

Ans.: Duncan, the Scottish King, has been listening to the report of the Sergeant about the battle between his generals Macbeth and Banquo and the rebel Macdonwald. Just as the rebel is finally defeated and his head is hung on the battlements, they get the news that the Norweyan lord, aided by the Thane of Cawdor has mounted "a fresh assault" on Scotland. Duncan thought that must have worried Macbeth and Banquo.

    ii.   *What is the function of the Sergeant's affirmative reply? Why do you think the dramatist uses that single word here?*

Ans.: The Sergeant's affirmative reply in fact functions as a negation of Duncan's assumption. It serves to highlight how far the king has misjudged the courage and loyalty of his generals.

The Sergeant is grievously wounded and probably feeling exhausted by his monologue earlier. Shakespeare's dramatic skill is such that he uses the single word to allow some breath to the Sergeant before he embarks on the new narrative. So that single word serves as evidence of Shakespeare's skill as well as empathy for his characters.

iii. *Why have been Macbeth and Banquo been compared to cannons? Why is such a comparison strange here?*

Ans.: Macbeth and Banquo have been compared to cannons because Shakespeare wanted to convey the complete destruction of the opposite army. His audience, familiar with the havoc that could be caused by cannons, would be able to imagine the sound and fury in the battlefield. So it is through the comparison that Shakespeare compensates for the lack of props on the Elizabethan stage.

The comparison is strange here because cannons were unknown to the Scotland of the 11th century, the time of Duncan's rule being from 1034 CE to 1040 CE. So the comparison is an anachronism here.

iv. *What motive does the speaker give to Macbeth and Banquo for their actions?*

Ans.: The Sergeant thinks that Macbeth and Banquo could have been motivated to act like doubly charged cannons because they wanted to ensure their wounds would tell of their fierce defence of Duncan. Another motive could be that they wanted the battle to be remembered in the same way as people remember Golgotha, the mountain where Jesus Christ was crucified. The Sergeant imputes the motive of unmatched violence in the battle by the allusion to the crucifixion which too was an incredibly violent act. This allusion is another anachronism because Christianity was yet to reach Duncan's Scotland.

v. *What is the dramatist's purpose in painting Macbeth as an eagle and a lion?*

Ans.: Both the eagle and the lion symbolise magnificence and power that inspire awe. Yet both these creatures are also predators. By comparing Macbeth to them, Shakespeare intends to convey to his audience that Macbeth is a powerful and magnificent figure on the battlefield, held in awe by all those who witness his exploits. Simultaneously, Shakespeare gives the image of Macbeth as a fierce hunter who swoops for his prey and goes for the kill with no remorse. There is an element of wildness and a spirit unfettered by civilisation imputed to Macbeth here.

4. Rosse: Ten thousand dollars to our general use.

Duncan: No more that Thane of Cawdor shall deceive

Our bosom interest. --- Go pronounce his present death,

And with his former title greet Macbeth.

Rosse: I'll see it done.

Duncan: What he hath lost, noble Macbeth hath won.

i. *Where are the speakers at this moment? Why have they come at this place?*

Ans.: Rosse and Duncan are in a camp, probably somewhere near the battlefield where Macbeth and Banquo were fighting against the rebel Macdonwald.

Duncan had followed his army and set up camp nearby to get news of the battle more quickly than he would have, had he stayed at the castle.

ii. *What news has Ross brought?*

Ans.: Ross has brought the news of Scottish victory against the Norwegian King who had mounted a new assault on the Scottish army immediately after Macbeth and Banquo had defeated Macdonwald. The treacherous Thane of

Cawdor had also joined forces with the Norwegians and the huge army had made the blood of the Scots run cold. There was a "dismal conflict" till Macbeth arrived on the scene and assured a Scottish victory by "Curbing his (Norway's) lavish spirit."

iii. *How does Duncan's decision affect the play's action?*

Ans.: Duncan decides to present the title of Cawdor to Macbeth once he returns from the battle. Ross is sent to convey the tidings to Macbeth who then starts believing in the truth of the Witches' greetings. He dashes off a letter to his wife and partner-in-crime, Lady Macbeth, about their desires being fulfilled in future. Lady Macbeth, knowing her husband's innate nobility of character, and unable to get power herself because of the social construct, decides to do her utmost to achieve their common ambition immediately. So Duncan's decision sets the course of the tragedy.

iv. *How does Shakespeare use the device of 'foreshadowing' in this extract?*

Ans.: The device of 'foreshadowing' is used in the ironical "What he hath lost, noble Macbeth hath won." Duncan bestows a traitor's title on Macbeth and sets off a chain of events he had never imagined. It is this title that ultimately leads to Macbeth's treacherous regicide. In effect, it gives an image of something that will happen in the future. So along with the land of Cawdor, Macbeth also gets the title of a future traitor. It also defines the tragedy of Macbeth's fall — from the pinnacle of glory that earns him this reward he falls into such depths of villainy that he loses it all. And so this single line foreshadows the battle being "lost and won".

v. *Violence in this scene leaves us awe-struck yet violence generally leaves us appalled. Why do you think we have this duality of response to violence?*

Ans.: In this scene, we see a glorification and sanction of violence in the descriptions of Macbeth as "Bellona's bridegroom", "brave Macbeth", "Valour's minion" and "O valiant cousin!". Yet Macdonwald and Thane of Cawdor, both equally good because the battles were fiercely contested, are killed as traitors. And so is Macbeth too in the end. This duality of response depends on the perspective – one is a 'traitor/terrorist/anti-national' from one lens and a 'freedom fighter/nationalist/patriot' from another. What may be a yardstick for distinguishing between the two is perhaps their 'vision' – whether it is a vision of restoration of order or a vision of personal gain that will result in anarchy. Macbeth deserves the label of a traitor in the play because his was the latter vision. As the Old Man says Scotland was reduced to anarchy under Macbeth. Yet we remain awe-struck by his indomitable spirit till the end and so he is also a tragic hero.

Act I, Sc. iii

i. **Multiple Choice Questions**

1. **"Aroint thee, witch!" the rump-fed ronyon cries. The word "rump-fed" conveys that the sailor's wife was quite ___________. Fill in the blank with the correct option.**

   a.   pampered

   b.   selfish

   c.   lean

   d.   scabby

2. **"I will drain him dry as hay:" – The first witch wanted to punish the sailor because ___________________. Choose the correct option to complete the sentence.**

   a.   it wanted to play with the sailor

   b.   it was filled with spite against him

   c.   it wanted to make the sailor's wife suffer

    d.   it wanted to take revenge

3.   **Choose the right option to match the given item in accordance with the play –**

    CAMEL : : DESERT : BARK : : _____________.

    a.   dog

    b.   kennel

    c.   ocean

    d.   lake

4.   **How many weeks will the witch make the sailor suffer?**

    a.   81 months

    b.   63 weeks

    c.   81 weeks

    d.   27 months

5.   **"The weird sisters, hand in hand,/Posters of the sea and land...." – The word 'posters' here mean _____________.**

    a.   couriers

    b.   swift travellers

    c.   carriers of mail

    d.   messengers

6.   **How many rounds do the witch make to wind up the charm?**

    a.   thrice

    b.   six times

    c.   twelve times

    d.   nine times

7.   **The witches are made to have beards because _____________________. Choose the right option to complete the sentence.**

   a.   Shakespeare wished to demonstrate that malignant forces have no gender

   b.   Shakespeare wanted to warn King James that both men and women were plotting to kill him

   c.   Shakespeare desired to make Banquo appear sympathetic towards them

   d.   Shakespeare was following the belief of his time that witches had beards

8. **The witches address Macbeth of their own volition while they speak to Banquo only after his invitation because _____________________. Choose the right option to complete the sentence.**

   a.   the witches had targeted Macbeth to fulfil their evil designs

   b.   the witches had prior knowledge of Banquo's scepticism about them

   c.   the witches were aware that Banquo would be able to evade their spell

   d.   the witches were aware of Macbeth's susceptibility to temptation

9. **Which of the following utterances convey that the witches were equivocaters?**

   a.   That he seems rapt withal

   b.   He shall live a man forbid

   c.   So foul and fair a day I have not seen

   d.   Stay, you imperfect speakers, tell me more

10. **"As thick as hail/Came post with post...." – Which of the following is similar to the literary device present in the given quote?**

   a.   The builders were working at a dizzy height

    b.   Not on thy sole but on thy soul, harsh Jew,/Thou makest thy knife keen

    c.   O my love's like a red, red rose, that's newly sprung in June

    d.   Parting is such sweet sorrow

11.   **"What, can the devil speak true?" – These words of Banquo are significant because _________________. Complete the sentence with the correct option.**

    a.   Banquo's conviction that the witches' words should be ignored remains unshaken

    b.   the witches being associated with the devil, take on more sinister proportions

    c.   the theme of good versus evil is brought out

    d.   they show that Banquo too is affected by their prophecies

12.   **"......why do you dress me/In borrow'd robes?" – Which of the following has the same literary device as in the given lines?**

    a.   He cannot buckle his distempered cause/Within the belt of rule.

    b.   Nothing in his life/Became him like the leaving it.

    c.   I have begun to plant thee and will labour/To make thee full of growing.

    d.   Will all great Neptune's ocean wash the blood/Clean from my hand?

13.   **Which of the following is an example of the theme of equivocation running through the play?**

    a.   .....who neither beg nor fear/Your favours nor your hate.

    b.   Not so happy, yet much happier.

    c.   The earth hath bubbles, as the water has,/And these are of them.

    d.   Were such things here as we do speak about?

14. "As happy prologues to the swelling act/Of the imperial theme." These lines refer to the sphere of _____________.

    a. poetry

    b. drama

    c. sports

    d. sculpture

15. The Weird Sisters call themselves "posters of the sea and land" because _____________________. Choose the correct option to complete the sentence.

    a. they carry messages over land and water

    b. they fly posters over land and water

    c. they use the mail to convey their messages

    d. they travel swiftly all over the earth

16. "....chance may crown me,/Without my <u>stir</u>." -- Choose the correct sentence that gives a meaning different to that of the underlined word.

    a. It is not possible to get a chance without any stir.

    b. Let's not stir up a hornet's nest.

    c. Did you notice a stir among the workers?

    d. The stir inconvenienced many.

17. "Time and the hour runs through the roughest day." – Choose the correct option that gives the meaning of this sentence.

    a. Even the best day comes to an end

    b. The time of the day is divided into hours

    c. Even the worst day comes to an end

    d. A day has only certain hours filled with trouble

18. Which of the following statements show Macbeth's keen desire for kingship?

    a.   Would they had stay'd!

    b.   And Thane of Cawdor too: went it not so?

    c.   The greatest is behind.

    d.   Present fears/Are less than horrible imaginings.

19. **What is the meaning of the underlined words in the context of the quoted sentence "That <u>trusted home</u>/Might yet enkindle you unto the crown...."?**

    a.   believed completely

    b.   disbelieved

    c.   domestic support

    d.   faithful wife

20. **Banquo is fence-sitting in this scene because _________________. Choose the right option to complete the sentence.**

    a.   he is eager for new honours that may come upon him

    b.   he feels Macbeth cannot be alienated openly

    c.   Macbeth has made his position very clear

    d.   Macbeth has put him on the horns of a dilemma

ii. Reference to Context

1. Second Witch: I'll give thee a wind.

   First Witch: Thou art kind.

   Third Witch: And I another.

   First Witch: I myself have all the other.

    i. *What impression of the Witches do you get from this scene?*

      Ans.: This scene gives an impression that the witches are people who are outcast from society and forced to live in the wilderness and survive on whatever they get. Such figures have always existed in folklore across the world. Living in isolation perhaps they do develop certain powers which they use to scare people who have dislocated them from usual human society. Shakespeare was first and foremost a humanist and this scene presents the witches with the usual human feelings of hunger, envy and revenge.

ii. *What angered the First Witch? Do you think her anger is justified?*

Ans.: The First Witch had ventured into a village and seen a "rump-fed ronyon" munching on chestnuts. The rude refusal of the sailor's wife to give the witch a few chestnuts angered the witch.

Yes, her anger is justified. The sailor's wife had plenty and it would not have harmed her to share a few to one asking for alms.

iii. *How does Shakespeare demonstrate the witches' powers in this scene? Give examples.*

Ans.: The First Witch declares that she will turn herself into a water-rat and board the sailor's ship, the Tiger. Then she will "drain him dry as hay" and ensure that he shall remain sleepless night and day. She will ensure that he will "dwindle, peak and pine" for nine times nine weary weeks. She will raise such tempestuous waves that the ship will be badly tossed about even though it cannot be driven off-course. So we see that basically the witches have some power over natural elements which when used with harmful intent, affect humans adversely.

iv. *How is the sailor's fate an instance of foreshadowing?*

Ans.: The witch declares that the sailor will suffer sleepless nights, will be so drained and exhausted that he will be merely existing and will pine for what is not. So shall Macbeth and so the sailor's fate is a foreshadowing of Macbeth's. Right after committing the murder, Macbeth tells his wife that since he had murdered sleep, "Macbeth shall sleep no more". Immediately after the discovery of Duncan's murder, he expresses his complete weariness of spirit in "The wine of life is drawn, and the mere lees/ Is left this vault to brag of." As he plunges into further violence, he says the famous "Tomorrow, and tomorrow, and tomorrow..." He knows he has stepped onto the "primrose way" from which there is no returning, and yet wishes fervently to turn the clock back.

v. *What kind of socio-economic structure is portrayed in the dialogues of the witches?*

Ans.: The witches reveal a society which was divided into the haves and the have-nots and there was no sympathy for the latter. One class of people, like sailors and merchants, had plenty but another class, perhaps represented by the witches, were often left to beg for food and shelter. The witches' dialogues reveal the bitterness and hatred felt by the latter class for the former. The haves dismissed the have-nots without any scruple and this lack of basic charity is reflected in the behaviour of the sailor's wife towards the Third Witch. Thus the Witches' dialogues reveal the socio-economic inequality that has remained down the ages.

2. Banquo: Good sir, why do you start, and seem to fear

Things that do sound so fair? – I'th'name of truth

Are ye fantastical, or that indeed

Which outwardly ye show? My noble partner

You greet with present grace, and great prediction

Of noble having, and of royal hope,

That he seems rapt withal: to me you speak not.

i. *Where are Banquo and Macbeth at present? What has made Macbeth 'start'?*

Ans.: Banquo and Macbeth are on their way to Forres where the Scottish king's palace is located. They have just come across the three Weird Sisters who are so withered and wild in their attire that they do not seem to be "inhabitants o' the earth".

They greeted Macbeth with the title of Thane of Cawdor and then declared that he would be "king hereafter." To his knowledge, the Thane of Cawdor was alive and so his being Cawdor was impossible. Again, so far as he knew, no one apart from his wife had any inkling of his ambition of succeeding to the Scottish throne. So these greetings startled Macbeth and his expression changed to one of apprehension.

ii. *Identify the play's theme as present in this extract. Quote the lines and explain.*

Ans.: One of the play's themes is 'appearance versus reality' and this is presented in this extract through Banquo's words – "Are ye fantastical, or that indeed/ Which outwardly ye show?" Banquo wonders whether the witches are figments of imagination or flesh and blood beings. The theme is mentioned in the opening scene of the play with the witches' words "Fair is foul and foul is fair" and reiterated throughout the play. In one of the most famous scenes of the play, Macbeth sees a dagger dripping blood. Though he realises it is a figment of his imagination, he is fascinated by the dagger's appearance. Lady Macbeth's words "Look like the innocent flower,/But be the serpent under't." and Duncan's "This castle hath a pleasant seat." are two more examples among others.

iii. *What appeal does Banquo make to the witches and how is it answered? What light does this appeal throw on his character?*

Ans.: Banquo appeals to the witches to reveal his future too. The witches hail him as "Lesser than Macbeth, and greater.", "Not so happy, yet much happier.", and "Thou shalt get kings, though thou be none:"

The appeal shows that Banquo, though sceptical of the witches and their ability to foretell the future, is not strong enough to resist the temptation they offer. It is probably true that he neither begs nor fears the witches' favours or hate. Yet he is as eager as the next man to know what the future holds for him.

iv.   *Why does Shakespeare present Banquo, and not Macbeth, as the one who will "get kings"?*

Ans.: In Shakespeare's source, Holinshed's *Chronicles*, Banquo is depicted as an accomplice in the murder of Duncan. Shakespeare, however, wrote *Macbeth* when James VI of Scotland had succeeded to the English throne after Queen Elizabeth I and had become James I of England. Shakespeare's theatre company became the King's Men with James I as his patron. With James on the throne, Shakespeare had a difficult moral as well as aesthetic challenge and he overcame both by making Banquo the begetter of kings. Since James claimed to be a descendant of Banquo, Shakespeare adroitly wove it into the text to please his sovereign and patron. Shakespeare also intended to present to his audience that one who uses violence to ascend the throne will not be the one to enjoy it. Therefore his aesthetic motive was also answered by this change of historical facts.

v.   *Macbeth calls the witches "you imperfect speakers". Why are these words significant for the play?*

Ans.: Macbeth calls the witches "imperfect speakers" because of but they speak in riddles, conveying part but never the whole truth. This use of ambiguous language to conceal the truth or avoid committing oneself is called equivocation. It is significant because it has a direct influence on the action of the play. The first meeting with the witches when he is greeted with "Thou shalt be king hereafter" lights the fire of Macbeth's dormant ambition and sets him on the course to hell and damnation.

When Macbeth re-visits the witches in a turmoil, again it is their equivocating words that give him a false sense of security. They tell him that he will not be defeated till Birnam Wood comes against him and "none of woman born" can harm him. By the time Macbeth realises that the "juggling fiends" must not be believed for they "palter with us in a double sense", it is too late.

3. Macbeth (Aside): Glamis, and Thane of Cawdor!

    The greatest is behind.

    (To Ross and Angus): Thanks for your pains.

    (To Banquo): Do you not hope your children shall be kings

    When those that gave the Thane of Cawdor to me

    Promis'd no less to them?

    i. *What news have Ross and Angus brought to Macbeth and Banquo?*

        Ans.: Ross and Angus have brought Macbeth and Banquo the news of how every post to Duncan bore "Thy praises in his kingdom's great defence". This made Duncan send them to invite both the generals to the king's presence and convey "from our royal master thanks". They have also been told by Duncan to greet Macbeth as Thane of not Glamis and Cawdor. When Macbeth wonders why he is being "dressed in borrow'd robes", Angus replies that the previous Thane of Cawdor had been executed as a traitor under royal orders.

    ii. *What does "the greatest is behind" imply? Why does Macbeth say the words in an aside?*

        Ans.: The phrase "the greatest is behind" implies the last prophecy of the witches that Macbeth will become the king of Scotland. Macbeth has been secretly nursing an ambition to be the king after Duncan since succession to the throne at that time was not hereditary. Macbeth's hopes of fulfilling his ambition rise when the first two prophecies of him becoming Glamis and Cawdor come true.

Macbeth says these words in an aside because his conscience tells him that his is "overvaulting ambition" and therefore immoral. He does not want Banquo to get wind of this at any cost.

iii.   *How does Banquo respond to Macbeth's question? What impression does the exchange leave on you?*

Ans.: Banquo responds quite firmly to Macbeth's question that if he were to trust the witches, his children would become kings only after Macbeth and that was too far in the future to contemplate. He advises Macbeth not to attach too much importance to what the "instruments of darkness" have said for they often mislead men into the wrong path by half-truths or "honest trifles".

The exchange makes it very clear that Banquo is sceptical of the "supernatural soliciting" while Macbeth, even understanding they "cannot be ill; cannot be good" falls prey to them because of the inherent vice of ambition in him. Shakespeare brings out the innate difference between the two men through this response of Banquo.

iv.   *Banquo is presented by Shakespeare as a foil to Macbeth. Give examples from this scene to support this view.*

Ans.: Banquo, unlike Macbeth, remains on his guard against the witches and their prophecies. Realising that Macbeth had fallen under the spell of the witches when two of their prophecies came true, Banquo warns Macbeth against their equivocations – "And oftentimes, to win us to our harm,/The instruments of darkness tell us truths,/Win us with honest trifles, to betray's/In deepest consequence." Unlike Macbeth, he is free from ambitions for kingship and is therefore able to take with equanimity what the witches reveal about him and his children. Unlike Macbeth, he is willing to let nature take its course and bring things to fruition.

v.   *"Fair is foul and foul is fair". Explain how Macbeth himself epitomises this in his character.*

Ans.: Macbeth is a tragic hero because of the very presence of the both good and bad in him. He is indeed "fair" for he has the virtues of courage and devotion to his duty, the quality of leadership and an indomitable spirit that enables him to surmount each obstacle or hardship that comes in the way of achieving his ambition. His powerful imagination acts as his conscience-keeper and each time he falters, he is goaded to action again. Yet, unfortunately, he has such an overpowering greed and ambition that though his thoughts "do shake (my) my single state of man", he murders the "one who is here in double trust....". As he continues with his murder spree, we find him becoming a conscience-less "fiend", a counterpart of the Devil himself. What could be more "foul"?

4.   Macbeth: If ill, why hath it given me earnest of success,

Commencing in a truth? I am Thane of Cawdor.

If good, why do I yield to that suggestion

Whose horrid image doth unfix my hair

And make my seated heart knock at my ribs,

Against the use of nature?

i.   *What is Macbeth debating in the given extract? Who is he debating with and why?*

Ans.: Macbeth is debating whether to believe or disbelieve the "supernatural soliciting" of the witches. Macbeth is soliloquising here. Since two of the witches' greetings (one of him becoming the thane of Glamis with Sinel's death and the other becoming the thane of Cawdor with the execution of the traitor Cawdor) have come true, he is tempted to believe that the third (he will become the king of Scotland) will be realised. He nurses the ambition of succeeding Duncan because Scotland at that time elected its monarch. It was not hereditary and as a first cousin Macbeth knew he had a good chance, especially since Malcolm was then a minor.

ii. *Why does the "horrid image" unseat Macbeth's heart?*

Ans.: The realisation of two of the witches' greetings makes Macbeth impatient, specially since the first two came in quick succession. Yet he fears that "vaulting ambition" will propel him into something that will arouse horror in one and all. He is using euphemism to refer to the murder of Duncan, the thought or "imaginings" of which is enough to make his hair stand on end in fear. Macbeth is aware of the wrong that would be done were he to do the deed. As "Bellona's bridegroom", he is used to violence on a battlefield where it is sanctioned by the state. But here, he will be using violence against the state itself in murdering Duncan. He knows that it will be an unforgivable act for Duncan, as said by Macbeth himself in the play (though not historically true), is a good and kind king. The image is horrifying because of the terror it unleashes in Macbeth's own heart and shakes his "single state of man".

iii. *What is meant by "Against the use of nature"?*

Ans.: The immediate meaning is of course that Macbeth, being Duncan's cousin and his thane would be committing the double crime of fratricide and regicide if he were to murder Duncan. His act would therefore be doubly unnatural. But there is a deeper meaning to this phrase and to understand it fully, we have to look into history. The tussle between the Catholics and the Protestants was rife in England and King James, a Protestant, suffered a few assassination attempts, the most infamous being the Gunpowder Plot. Shakespeare's family was closet-Catholic and perhaps Shakespeare took this opportunity to assure his monarch James that he believed in the doctrine of the "divine right of kings". The phrase therefore hits at the basic conflict raging in Macbeth the character and *Macbeth* the play – what makes Macbeth's ambition wrong/unnatural is that it forces him to over-ride natural order of things. And Shakespeare makes it clear to his audience that were they to instigate further plots against their anointed king, they would face the same tragedy as Macbeth.

iv. *This soliloquy ends with "And nothing is, but what is not." – Which of the play's themes does this line refer to? Explain briefly.*

Ans.: The quoted line refers to the theme of appearance versus reality that reverberates through the play. It is a paradoxical statement echoing the witches' words in the opening scene of the play -- "Fair is foul and foul is fair".

Nothing but future kingship is real for Macbeth, but since this 'reality' exists only in his imagination, it is merely 'appearance' – what 'is' in his mind 'is not' in the real world. This confusion between the real and the appearance of the real puts Macbeth under tremendous psychological stress. Though mere speculation in his mind, the very thought of murder is enough to unman him. He realises that his logic and reasoning are being usurped by his imagination which urges him towards usurping the crown. Its significance thus lies in underlining the tragedy that befalls Macbeth for it is his powerful imagination that goads him and then destroys him.

v. *Which of Shakespeare's skills is apparent in this speech? Explain your choice.*

Ans.: Shakespeare's skill in the art of characterisation is apparent in this speech. In order to elevate Macbeth from a bloody villain to a tragic hero, he has to portray Macbeth in a way that makes him earn the audience's respect if not their sympathy. So he imbues Macbeth with an imagination that constantly shows him the consequences of his actions. There is no doubt that Macbeth has a moral compass which is revealed in the very beginning of this soliloquy – "This supernatural soliciting/Cannot be ill, cannot be good:...". It is this compass that unnerves him with the "horrid image" and "shakes so my (his) single state of man...". Shakespeare uses this soliloquy to portray Macbeth's genuine fear of being immoral and that lends a sensitivity to Macbeth which endears him to the audience. At every turn of the play's action, we find it is this emotional rejection of his physical actions that make Macbeth a tragic hero.

Act I, Sc. iv

i. **Multiple Choice Questions**

1. **Choose the correct option to fill in the blank in accordance with the text –**

   LIEGE : KING : : SUBJECT : _______________.

   a. vessel

   b. vassal

   c. crony

   d. kinsman

2. **Cawdor meets his death with a noble dignity that Malcolm finds surprising. What does this reflect of the then society?**

   a. Society was orthodox in its beliefs

   b. Society put people into boxes

   c. Society was similar to modern society

   d. Society treated traitors ignominiously

3. **What do you think makes Cawdor repent his treachery?**

   a. Fear of being executed

   b. Hope of being pardoned

    c.   Desire for a reprisal

    d.   Hunger for praise

4.   **What does Duncan mean by "mind's construction"?**

    a.   thoughts

    b.   feelings

    c.   brain

    d.   emotions

5.   **"The sin of my ingratitude even now/Was heavy on me." – What is the significance of this line?**

    a.   The line echoes the play's theme of appearance versus reality

    b.   Malcolm is made the Prince of Cumberland to expiate this sin

    c.   Macbeth will bear the weight of being an ingrate

    d.   The line echoes the play's theme of reversal of fortunes

6.   **Fill in the blank by choosing the correct option in accordance with the text –**

   DUNCAN : FARMER : : MACBETH ______________.

    a.   TREE

    b.   SHRUB

    c.   CROP

    d.   PLANT

7.   **What is Duncan's reaction to his "plenteous joys"?**

    a.   He gives gifts to everyone

    b.   He cannot control his smiles

    c.   He weeps

    d.   He embraces everyone around

8. **What is the relation between Forres and Inverness?**

    a.   Both are places with castles

    b.   Both are names of battlefields

    c.   Both are places where Duncan set up camp

    d.   Both are names of Duncan's castles

9. **"....let that be/Which the eye fears...." – What does Macbeth mean by these words?**

    a.   Macbeth is afraid to see the murder of Duncan but is not averse to it happening

    b.   Macbeth does not wish to see Duncan's murder and wishes to stop thinking of it

    c.   The sight of Duncan's dead body will be painful and so Macbeth does not wish to see it

    d.   The eye fears the very thought of murder and so Macbeth does not want to do it

10. **COMMENDATIONS: _______________:: STARS: CONSTELLATIONS. Choose the correct alternative to fill in the blank as per the text.**

    A.   FEAST

    B.   CEREMONY

    C.   APPLAUSE

    D.   BANQUET

ii. Reference to context

1.   Malcolm: Nothing in his life

     Became him like the leaving it; he died

     As one that had been studied in his death

     To throw away the dearest thing he owed,

     As 'twere a careless trifle.

Duncan: There's no art

To find the mind's construction in the face

He was a gentleman on whom I built

An absolute trust ----

i. *Where are Malcolm and Duncan at this point of time? Who are they talking about and why?*

Ans.: Malcolm and Duncan are inside a room of Duncan's castle at Forres.

They are talking about the treacherous Thane of Cawdor who had assisted the invading King of Norway against Scotland. The Norwegian king had been defeated by Macbeth and Banquo and the Scottish army had demanded a ransom for his release. The Thane of Cawdor, however, had been sentenced to death and executed under the King's orders.

ii. *Why does Malcom say "Nothing in his life/Became him like the leaving it"?*

Ans.: The Thane of Cawdor had, surprisingly, been very calm and collected at his death. He had frankly confessed his treachery and begged Duncan's pardon. He faced death with such stoicism and dignity that it surprised Malcolm. It seemed he had studied how to treat life, the most precious thing, with complete indifference and feel no regret at losing it. This won Malcolm's admiration and is another instance of the truth of "Fair is foul and foul is fair."

iii. *Which of the play's themes are found in this extract?*

Ans.: The theme of appearance versus reality that runs through the play before the regicide is committed is evident in Duncan's words "There's no art/To find the mind's construction in the face." Duncan understands that it is not always possible to understand a person's thoughts by seeing his facial expressions. Just as Duncan had failed to read Cawdor, he fails to read Lady Macbeth and Macbeth when he goes to their castle. Another famous example of this theme is Lady Macbeth telling Macbeth to look like a flower but be the serpent under it.

iv. *"He was a gentleman on whom I built/An absolute trust." – How is this statement significant in the context of the play?*

Ans.: Duncan had bestowed complete trust on Cawdor and failing to read him correctly, been terribly deceived. He then bestows the same unquestioning trust on Macbeth and pays the price for it with his life. Macbeth becomes a tragic hero because he is haunted by the fact that his action has broken the sacred bond of trust between a sovereign and his subject. Yet even repentance is useless because he realises that he cannot turn the clock back – "What is done, cannot be undone."

v. *What quality of Duncan becomes apparent in his speech here?*

Ans.: This speech shows Duncan to be a poor judge of character and easily impressed by outward show. Despite his age, he shows himself as a man without the wisdom needed to rule a kingdom. He has been betrayed by one whom he had trusted completely and his folly lies in that he does not learn from his mistake. He again trusts someone completely and not only does he pay dearly for his mistake but his whole kingdom does.

2. Macbeth: The service and the loyalty I owe,

In doing it, pays itself. Your Highness' part

Is to receive our duties: and our duties

Are to your throne and state, children and servants,

Which do but what they should, by doing everything

Safe toward your love and honour.

Duncan: Welcome hither;

I have begun to plant thee, and will labour

To make thee full of growing.

i.   *What were Duncan's words that occasioned Macbeth's response?*

Ans.: Duncan has just expressed his sense of guilt at not being able to go himself and convey his gratitude to Macbeth for the service he has rendered to his king and country. Duncan conveys that Macbeth deserves much more than he can give and that makes him regretful. In fact, such is his regret that he wishes Macbeth had less merit for then he could have given sufficient recompense. It is this fulsome tribute of Duncan's that occasions Macbeth's response here.

ii.   *Which of the play's many messages does Macbeth's words reflect?*

Ans.: One of the messages of this play, written right after King James survived the Gunpowder Plot, is the divine right of kings and duty of the subjects towards their sovereign and citizens towards the state. Shakespeare very clearly wished to reiterate to his audience that the sovereign was God's anointed deputy and that doing their duty towards their king was its own reward. The king had the right to command and expect complete obedience from his subjects and any one deviating from the king's command was a traitor deserving the death sentence. Since Macbeth establishes himself as king by claiming Duncan's life, he committed treason against his king and country. So despite his heroism, he has to die at the end of the play for Shakespeare to enforce his message on the audience.

iii.   *Explain the metaphorical comparison in Duncan's words in the extract.*

Ans.: A metaphor is an indirect comparison between two dissimilar objects to bring out a point of similarity. Here, the comparison is between the gardener and a plant to establish the point of nurture and growth. Duncan uses the metaphor of gardening to elaborate on his relationship to Macbeth. He claims to be the gardener who has planted Macbeth and will work hard to nourish the plant so Macbeth attains full growth.

iv. *Do you think Duncan is impartial in his praise? Give reasons for your answer.*

Ans.: Duncan is certainly not impartial in his praise for he first singles out Macbeth for effusive words of gratitude. He greets Banquo almost as an afterthought and embraces him. His words – "Noble Banquo,/That hast no less deserved ....." -- are not charged with the emotion as evident in the fulsome praise of Macbeth – "O worthiest cousin!/The sin of my ingratitude....". And yet, all the reports that he has got from the messengers convey that Banquo played no less a role in defeating Scotland's enemies. Banquo's awareness of Duncan's partiality is rather starkly revealed in the somewhat curt response to Duncan "There if I grow,/The harvest is your own."

v. *Why is this extract highly ironical?*

Ans.: This extract is highly ironical because it highlights the false security that Duncan envelops himself in. A gardener is rarely betrayed by a plant he has nourished to full growth but there are instances when the plants grow into trees that bear no fruit. The same thing happens here. Duncan the gardener thinks that his nurture or "absolute trust" in Macbeth will earn him a devoted servant. Unfortunately, Duncan is betrayed by Macbeth and it almost seems he is betrayed by his own hand. The irony of course lies in that Duncan is completely oblivious of his future.

3. Banquo: There if I grow

The harvest is your own.

Duncan: My plenteous joys

Wanton in fulness, seek to hide themselves

In drops of sorrow. --- Sons, kinsmen, Thanes,

And you whose places are the nearest, know,

We will establish our estate upon

Our oldest, Malcolm; whom we name hereafter

The Prince of Cumberland......

i. *What "harvest" is Banquo referring to and why?*

Ans.: Duncan has welcomed Macbeth with the "plant" metaphor and said he looked forward to seeing Macbeth blossoming under him. Duncan assures Banquo that he too deserves "no less" than Macbeth because he has done as much as Macbeth. Duncan expresses his gratitude "....let me infold thee,/And hold thee to my heart." Banquo continues the "plant" metaphor with his words with the use of the word "harvest".

Shakespeare continues the same metaphor through Banquo's words to emphasise the proverbial saying "as you sow, so shall you reap." As a ruler, Duncan makes the mistake of bestowing "absolute trust" on Macbeth and reaps the reward of death. Shakespeare is making it clear to his audience that kings and rulers do not have the luxury of trusting someone completely. This was specially true in Shakespeare's times that were full of intrigue.

ii. *Why does Duncan refer to tears in this extract?*

Ans.: Duncan is so overwhelmed by his generals' reassuring words of loyalty that his cup of joy brims over. The tears that spring to his eyes and flow down his cheeks are expressions of his joy and not sorrow that they are usually associated with. Shakespeare wants to portray Duncan as a symbol of 'benign grace' here. This would make his murder all the more unjust and unpardonable.

The tears also remind us that "joy and woe are woven fine" in the tapestry of life.

iii. *Why do you think Duncan bestows the title of the Prince of Cumberland on Malcolm?*

Ans.: Scotland at the time of Duncan was not a hereditary monarchy and the Prince of Cumberland (like the modern-day Prince of Wales) was heir to the throne. The rebellions in his kingdom told Duncan that his death would probably plunge Scotland into chaos as thanes fought to win supremacy and the crown. Duncan perhaps sought to eliminate this unnecessary civil war and ensure that his own line would continue ruling by making Malcolm the Prince of Cumberland.

iv. *What is the effect of these words on Macbeth?*

Ans.: Duncan's sudden announcement of Malcolm as the heir apparent puts Macbeth in a spot. It must be remembered that monarchy in Macbeth's time was not hereditary and as Duncan's first cousin, Macbeth perhaps had a chance to the throne ("chance may crown me,/ Without my stir."). But with Malcolm as the declared heir, Macbeth realises he either has to forget his ambition or else do something to cross the hurdle. He takes the decision to murder "The eye wink at the hand" at this point of time, and though he "fears....to see" he wants it done "yet let that be."

v. *How would you estimate Duncan's character from his words in this extract?*

Ans.: This extract reveals a side to Duncan's character that is often overlooked because of the concentrated attention on Macbeth. Duncan intends the Prince of Cumberland to be the title of the Scottish heir apparent, but there is no such title in Scottish history. Duncan's words "We will establish our estate" therefore goes against Scottish convention of electing the monarch and shows Duncan's ambition of having his line continue on the Scottish throne. Duncan is also aware that his declaration may not be liked by others and so he assures that he will shower "signs of nobleness" on others as well. So Duncan is not as naïve and gullible as he seems to be.

4. Macbeth (aside): ....Stars, hide your fires!

Let not light see my black and deep desires;

The eye wink at the hand; yet let that be,

Which the eye fears, when it is done, to see. (Exit)

Duncan: True, worthy Banquo: he is full so valiant,

And in his commendations I am fed;

It is a banquet to me. Let's after him,

Whose care is gone before to bid us welcome:

It is a peerless kinsman.

i. *Why is Macbeth's speech here important with regard to Lady Macbeth's assessment of her husband?*

Ans.: Lady Macbeth has earlier portrayed Macbeth as a man who would do "holily" what he wants "highly", who has too much of the "milk of human kindness" to fulfil his ambition using foul means. Yet this speech proves that her estimate of his character is not completely correct. He does "fear" to take the unholy path but here, he makes a deliberate choice to do evil for he confesses that his desires are "black". He also takes the decision to commit the murder even though he is averse to it -- "The eye wink at .... to see." This speech remains significant in the long run because it proves that the decision to murder Duncan was not instigated or prompted by either the witches or Lady Macbeth. The "black and deep desires" reside in him already.

ii. *What does the expression "The eye wink at the hand" mean? What is its significance?*

Ans.: Shakespeare uses this expression to portray Macbeth's unwillingness to be witness to the dreadful deed of murdering Duncan. He wants his own eye to "wink" or blind itself to what his hand would do, that is murder from which he recoils.

The significance of the expression lies in the fact that it expresses his instinctive repulsion at the imminent deed; he does not want to be a witness to his own action. It foreshadows his mental turmoil before the murder because he truly is never at ease with the thought of taking Duncan's life through such treacherous means.

iii. *What are some of the "commendations" that Duncan refers to here? How do they contrast with the words spoken by Macbeth?*

Ans.: The "commendations" Duncan refers to here are the fulsome praises that the messengers such as Ross and Angus have brought to Duncan from the battlefield. Macbeth has been "valour's minion" defending his king and country against the rebel Macdonwald. He has been "Bellona's bridegroom" and vanquished the Norwegian king Sweno who now "craves compensation."

The violent acts on the battlefield are praiseworthy despite their very nature. And yet violence committed inside the castle is just the opposite of being "commendations", it becomes an act of treachery. Macbeth's words reveal his awareness of the fact that he cannot commit the murder openly because it is not condemnable act and so he wants the stars to "hide their fires".

iv. *Why do you think Shakespeare has made this contrast?*

Ans.: Shakespeare perhaps wanted to make a distinction in the nature of violence. Whenever violence is a weapon for defence of state or country, it is morally sanctioned. But when violence is used to forward an individual or a group's greed or agenda, it must be condemned. Shakespeare wrote this play in 1606 just a year after the Gunpowder Plot that failed to assassinate King James I. Perhaps it was uppermost in Shakespeare's mind while writing this play and as a believer in the "divine right of kings" doctrine, perhaps he took this opportunity to warn those trying to use violent means to bring a change. He wishes to make it very clear that regicide is an unpardonable act.

v. *Duncan calls Macbeth "a peerless kinsman." How far do you agree with him? Give reasons to support your answer.*

Ans.: So far as Macbeth's valour on the battlefield is concerned, Macbeth is indeed peerless. Unfortunately, being a party to Macbeth's thoughts, I cannot agree with the praise implied in this epithet used by Duncan. Macbeth has already expressed his ambition of being the king as well as his decision to murder to fulfil this ambition. Thus, Macbeth does become "peerless" for never before perhaps has someone coming in triple trust – as a cousin, as a king, and as a guest – been so cruelly deprived of life. The expression becomes highly ironical in the context of the play.

Act I, Sc. v

i. Multiple Choice Questions

1. "Whiles I stood rapt in the wonder of it, came missives from the king….". The word 'missives' here means _________________. Choose the correct option to fill in the blank.

   a. letters

   b. warnings

   c. recommendations

   d. messengers

2. What does Macbeth mean when he says, "Lay it to thy heart…."?

   a. Let it die in your heart

   b. Keep it a secret in your heart

    c.   Keep it forever in your heart

    d.   None of the above

3. **"Yet do I fear thy nature...." Choose the correct option to complete the sentence according to the text. Lady Macbeth fear her husband's nature because ___________________________.**

    a.   Macbeth has too generous a nature

    b.   it will permit taking the dangerous path

    c.   it will prevent him from being holy

    d.   Macbeth is unscrupulous by nature

4. **Choose the correct option to fill in the blank in accordance with the text –**

    SPIRITS : EAR : : ______________ TONGUE

    a.   CHASTISE

    b.   SWORD

    c.   VALOUR

    d.   BLADE

5. **Choose the correct option that matches the literary device used in "the fatal entrance of Duncan".**

    a.   The night has been unruly

    b.   Love is an ideal, marriage is real

    c.   The wipers squeaked in protest

    d.   Every dog has his day

6. **The 'hand and eye' imagery used by Macbeth earlier is repeated in one of the given options. Choose the correct one.**

    a.   ..... bear welcome in your eye,/Your hand, your tongue....

    b.   To alter favour ever is to fear

    c.   That my keen knife see not the wound it makes

    d.   Your face, my Thane, is as a book

7.   **What is meant by "To beguile the time/Look like the time"?**

    a.   Behave in manner appropriate to the time so that time itself is deceived

    b.   To deceive time, follow your instincts

    c.   To pass the present time, have a happy expression on your face

    d.   Behave such that time is not fooled

8.   **Lady Macbeth proves better than Duncan in _____________. Choose the right option to fill in the blank.**

    a.   reading faces

    b.   studying art

    c.   praising falsely

    d.   creating impressions

ii. Reference to context

1.   Lady Macbeth: Thou wouldst be great;

    Art not without ambition, but without

    The illness should attend it: what thou wouldst highly

    That wouldst thou holily; wouldst not play false,

    And yet wouldst wrongly win; thou'dst have, great Glamis

    That which cries "Thus thou must do", if thou have it,

    And that which rather thou dost fear to do,

    Than wishest should be undone.

    i.   *What prompts Lady Macbeth to say these words?*

    Ans.: Lady Macbeth has been reading the letter Macbeth sent informing her about the witches' prophecies. They set her hopes soaring since she was also an ambitious lady.

But she was more impatient than Macbeth and wanted the crown immediately. However she knew that Macbeth would not easily agree to taking the short cut to the throne. She then soliloquises on the traits in Macbeth's character that will hinder the realisation of their ambition.

ii. *What picture of Macbeth's character is portrayed here?*

Ans.: Macbeth, according to the extract here, is ambitious and desires greatness but lacks the firmness of purpose needed to achieve greatness and the will to pay the price for it. Macbeth desires things out of his bounds but shies away from taking any foul means to achieve it. Macbeth is wary of the consequences of actions and fears reprisal but he would not reject the opportunity to be king if someone else took Duncan out of his way. So Macbeth seems a rather weak character mentally at this point of time. His physical courage is without question but his moral strength is questionable. The struggle between his desires and moral conscience is made clear in this soliloquy and it is this vulnerability that ultimately makes him a tragic hero.

iii. *What is the significance of this soliloquy in the context of the play?*

Ans.: This soliloquy makes people think of Macbeth as a rather weak character who has to be bolstered by Lady Macbeth to fulfil their ambition of ruling Scotland. Its significance in the context of the play lies in the fact that it makes people misinterpret Lady Macbeth's role in the assassination. It paints her blacker, stronger mentally and more evil than she actually is. The last lines of the soliloquy "Hie thee hither,/That I may pour my spirits in thine ear;/And chastise with the valour of my tongue/All that impedes thee from the golden round....." specially heightens the impression of Lady Macbeth being more powerful mentally than Macbeth. But as the play progresses, we realise that it is just a façade of strength.

iv. *What kind of reception does Lady Macbeth give to Macbeth on his arrival? What does Macbeth's reaction convey about him?*

Ans.: Lady Macbeth greets her husband in ecstatic joy. She calls him "Greater than both, by the all-hail hereafter!" taking for granted that they will be reigning Scotland sooner rather than later. She tells him that his letter has given wings to her imagination and transported her to the future. Her words paint the picture of a perfect power couple.

Macbeth, however, is rather subdued in response. He is worried about the consequences of Duncan's visit and his face reveals the battle between doubt and desire raging in his mind.

v. *Do you think Lady Macbeth has painted a true picture of her husband? Give reasons to support your answer.*

Ans.: Yes, Lady Macbeth has read her husband very correctly. We have already seen how eager Macbeth is to believe in what the witches say. We have seen how disappointed he is that they vanish when he wants them to tell him more – "Would they had stayed!". That Macbeth is keen on becoming the king is apparent in his aside "The greatest lies behind" and the way he dashes off the letter to Lady Macbeth. But his misgivings also find voice in "This supernatural soliciting cannot be ill; cannot be good....". He feels guilty at the very thought of committing treason and so begs Lady Macbeth to keep the letter's contents secret. As the action progresses, at every step we find him plagued by his conscience because he failed to overcome the temptation of ambition. So yes, Lady Macbeth has correctly painted her husband's picture.

2. Lady Macbeth: Give him tending.

He brings great news. The raven himself is hoarse,

That croaks the fatal entrance of Duncan

Under my battlements. Come, you Spirits

That tend on mortal thoughts, unsex me here,

And fill me, from the crown to the toe, top-full

Of direst cruelty!

i.   *Who has to be given "tending" and why?*

Ans.: One of the fellow-servants of the messenger had raced to the Macbeths' castle to inform about the king's imminent arrival. He needed "tending" because he was so short of breath as to be almost dead. He was so breathless due to the hard riding that he could barely say the necessary words. Lady Macbeth ordered him to be specially cared for since he had brought such good news.

ii.   *What does the expression "fatal entrance of Duncan" mean here? Why is the mention of the "raven" significant?*

Ans.: The expression "fatal entrance" is a transferred epithet and conveys the meaning that once Duncan enters the castle, it will prove fatal for him. In other words, Lady Macbeth conveys that Duncan will not leave the castle alive.

The raven is a bird of ill-omen and its croaking to herald Duncan's arrival is a sign to Lady Macbeth that even nature is announcing the imminent death of Duncan.

iii.   *Which element/theme of the play recurs in this extract?*

Ans.: One of the overriding elements of the play is supernaturalism. The play opens with the witches and their incantation "Fair is foul and foul is fair/Hover through the fog and the filthy air." This establishes the supernatural atmosphere that is further enhanced by the meeting of Macbeth and Banquo and their predications, two of which are uncannily fulfilled. Here, too Lady Macbeth mentions the raven croaking Duncan's fatal entrance has an eerie ring. Her invocation to the spirits to remove the last drops of femininity in her and fill her from top to toe with direst cruelty is a direct reference to the supernatural.

iv. *Which of the two qualities does Lady Macbeth reveal here – cruelty or vulnerability? Explain your view.*

Ans.: Lady Macbeth reveals here the quality of 'vulnerability'. Often labelled as the fourth witch by critics, this speech demonstrates how terribly wrong that label is. Lady Macbeth has to call on supernatural powers to fortify herself before she can "chastise" Macbeth with the "valour" of her tongue. Had she not been vulnerable to tender feelings of a woman, she would not have needed the spirits to "unsex" her. The very fact that she has to make this appeal so that she may behave in a more masculine manner is evidence of her vulnerability.

v. *How does Shakespeare break conventions in this speech?*

Ans.: This speech is one where Shakespeare deals more with Elizabethan and Jacobean conventions in England rather than 11th century Scotland. English society of Shakespeare's time was definitely patriarchal despite Queen Elizabeth's long reign. Lady Macbeth has to "unsex" herself to get the feeling of power in her. The phrase "direst cruelty" coupled with "unsex" gives an impression of toxic masculinity. On the other hand, Shakespeare could be trying to convey how women with strong personalities like Lady Macbeth must have felt stifled by the conventions forced on them because of their gender. Through such associations perhaps Shakespeare is sending signals to his audience that mindsets must change, that women too have desire for power and ambition and that should not be scorned as unfeminine. How far ahead of his times was Shakespeare!

3. Lady Macbeth: Your face, my Thane, is a book, where men

   May read strange matters. To beguile the time

   Look like the time; bear welcome in your eye,

Your hand, your tongue: look like the'innocent flower

But be the serpent under't. He that's coming

Must be provided for; and you shall put

This night's great business into my dispatch;

Which shall to all our nights and days to come,

Give solely sovereign sway and masterdom.

i. *What does Lady Macbeth read in her husband's face? What does this tell you about her?*

Ans.: Macbeth's face is like an open book which Lady Macbeth reads easily. She sees the expressions of doubt and fear battling with desire in his face as he contemplates becoming the Scottish king and ruling over the land. She realises that he had to be guarded in expression else his face would betray him by revealing his thoughts.

This shows that Lady Macbeth was aware of her husband's deficiencies and was astute enough to warn him about his drawback.

ii. *How does her statement contradict Duncan's statement made earlier?*

Ans.: Duncan had said earlier that "There's no art/To find the mind's construction in the face....". Lady Macbeth's statement that Macbeth's face was like an open book is a contradiction of Duncan's earlier statement. That Duncan has little ability to understand men's characters is evident because both gentlemen on whom he bestows his "absolute trust" betray him. Lady Macbeth on the other hand, is much sharper in intelligence and is thus able to read the expressions flitting across her husband's face immediately.

iii. *Explain "To beguile the time/Look like the time."*

Ans.: Lady Macbeth knows that if they are to succeed in their plot, they must be very careful about their words and actions. Since she could read her husband's face so easily, she feared others coming with Duncan would suspect something amiss unless Macbeth was careful. So she advises Macbeth to behave in the way a thane welcoming his sovereign to his castle would. Macbeth should play the genial host, happy and gracious in his behaviour towards Duncan and his retinue. She tells Macbeth that to deceive people into thinking that all was well at present, he had to behave according to the dictates of the current situation. The current situation demanded he behave with a cheerful dignity as befitting a victorious general welcoming his commander, the king.

iv.   *What Biblical allusion is found in this extract?*

Ans.: The imagery of the flower and serpent immediately brings forth the picture of the Garden of Eden where Eve was tempted by Satan disguised as a serpent. This allusion to a Biblical story foreshadows how Macbeth will turn into a "hell-hound" later in the play. In the present scene, the imagery turns the "pleasant seat" of the castle of Inverness into another Eden where tragedy is about to happen. This one imagery raises Macbeth's tragedy to epic proportions signalling that greed and overvaulting ambition leads to a descent into hell and eternal damnation.

v.   *Why does Lady Macbeth wish to control the events that night?*

Ans.: Lady Macbeth knows that Macbeth's nature "is too full o'th'milk of human kindness". Reading his facial expressions, she knows he is still undecided about the deed and is warring with his conscience. She fears that he may back out at a critical juncture of the assassination attempt and leave them exposed to the charge of treason. Unable to depend on him to handle the nitty-gritties of their plot to avoid the least suspicion, she takes over command of the events that night.

Act I, Sc vi

i. **Multiple Choice Questions**

1. **"The air nimbly and sweetly recommends itself....." – Which of the following gives the correct meaning of the line?**

    a. There is a strong and sweet wind blowing

    b. There is a pleasant breeze around

    c. One hopes to feel the sweet-smelling wind

    d. There is strong breeze blowing

2. **What figure of speech is found in "pendant bed"?**

    a. simile

    b. metaphor

    c. transferred epithet

    d. oxymoron

3. **What is meant by the words "procreant cradle"?**

    a. rocking bed

    b. nestlings

    c. nest where hatchlings are growing

    d. the earth

4. **"The air is <u>delicate.</u>" – Give the meaning of the underlined word.**

    a. fragile

    b. weak

    c. delicious

    d. pleasant

5. **Lady Macbeth refers to herself and Macbeth as "hermits" because _________________. Choose the right option to complete the sentence.**

    a. they depend on the alms given by the king

    b. they have no stability in their lives

    c. they will always pray for the welfare of the king

    d. they have renounced their loyalty

6. **The word "audit" used by Lady Macbeth implies that _________________. Choose the right option to complete the sentence.**

    a. she had knowledge of commercial transactions

    b. she was responsible for Macbeth's business

    c. she was a lady of wealth and means

    d. she had business qualities

ii. **Reference to context**

1. Banquo: This guest of summer,

    The temple-haunting martlet, does approve,

    By his lov'd mansionry, that the heaven's breath

    Smells wooingly here: no jutty, frieze,

    Buttress, nor coign of vantage, but this bird

    Hath made his pendant bed and procreant cradle:

    Where they most breed and haunt, I have observed,

    The air is delicate.

    i. *How is the atmosphere of this scene different from the last few scenes?*

        Ans.: The play had opened with thunder and lightning and the presence of witches onstage. This supernatural atmosphere had then been replaced by the grim atmosphere of the battlefield with the clash of swords, severed heads hung on battlements and unapologetic violence. For the first time, we find a lighter atmosphere of pleasant summer weather where the "gentle senses" are soothed by sweet air and the fragrance of flowers borne by the "heaven's breath". Banquo's reference to "heaven's breath" and "procreant cradle" imbue the castle with an air of peace and health.

ii.   *What is the purpose of this scene?*

Ans.: The purpose of this scene is to highlight the treachery of the Macbeths. The castle has a "pleasant seat" and Duncan enters it unsuspecting of the fate that lies in wait for him inside. Banquo's speech has images of new life and growth "pendant bed and procreant cradle" but Lady Macbeth has already said that the raven has grown hoarse croaking "the fatal entrance" of Duncan. This is the only scene in which one breathes freely and naturally and it gives the audience a chance to relax before being plunged headlong into the breathless cycle of murder and mayhem till the very end of the play. The scene shows the deceptiveness of appearances and how easily concord may be replaced by discord.

iii.   *What makes the mention of the "martlet" ironical?*

Ans.: The martlet has been used by Shakespeare to convey a sense of sanctity to the castle because generally the martlet would build its nest in the nooks and crannies of churches. Ironically, the Macbeths violate this sanctity when they murder Duncan and his guards. Also, the image of nesting and babies that is associated here with the martlet is symbolic of life and growth in safety but the castle is one where Duncan meets his death and his children, Malcolm and Donalbain are forced to flee their country. Therefore, the mention of the martlet is very ironical.

iv.   *How does Duncan greet Lady Macbeth?*

Ans.: Lady Macbeth greets Duncan at the castle doors. Duncan graciously acknowledges the trouble she has taken to welcome him and thanks her for the love she shows through her actions. On a lighter note, he says that sometimes he finds the trouble people take to express their love rather overwhelming. And yet he is grateful for it. He tells Lady Macbeth that he has just demonstrated how she should ask God to reward Duncan for the pains she has undertaken and so she should be grateful to Duncan for giving her the opportunity to undergo some trouble on his behalf.

v.   *What estimate of Lady Macbeth's character do you make from this scene?*

Ans.: Lady Macbeth is accomplished in the art of genteel hospitality. Like a true and faithful lady of the castle, she rushes to the castle gates to meet her king and welcomes him warmly. Not for a split second does she betray her anxiety about the success of their plan to commit regicide. She plays the role of a gracious hostess without a single misstep and wins over Duncan's heart. Well-versed in courtly language as well as the art of deception, she gives all the correct responses to Duncan and earns his complete trust. She does not seem to be filled with direst cruelty from top to toe and she is certainly the epitome of femininity in this scene.

2.   Lady Macbeth: All our service,

In every point twice done, and then done double,

Were poor and single business, to contend

Against those honours deep and broad, wherewith

Your Majesty loads our house: for those of old,

And the late dignities heap'd up to them,

We rest your hermits.

Duncan: Where's the Thane of Cawdor?

We cours'd him at the heels, and had a purpose

To be his purveyor: but he rides well;

And his love, sharp as his spur, hath holp him

To his home before us.

i. *What is the meaning of **late** in the phrase "late dignities"? Why does Lady Macbeth refer to herself and Macbeth as "hermits"?*

Ans.: The word **late** here carries the meaning of recent and the phrase "recent dignities" conveys the honours bestowed recently on Macbeth by Duncan, specially the title of the Thane of Cawdor and the royal visit to Inverness.

Hermits were almsmen in the king's entourage and they were hired to pray for the welfare of the king and his men. Here, Lady Macbeth means to convey that like his almsmen, both she and Macbeth would pray for Duncan's welfare in gratitude for all the honours he has heaped upon them.

ii. *How do Lady Macbeth's words echo one of the themes of the play?*

Ans.: One of the themes of the play is 'equivocation' and these words of Lady Macbeth are an excellent example of the theme. We have already seen how Lady Macbeth is ready to take foul means to take the crown. Macbeth wants to be king but he would rather it be "holily"; such moral scruples do not hinder her. So when she expresses her gratitude in this speech, we are made aware of how false the words are. Just like the fulfilment of two of the witches' prophecies make Macbeth believe that the third would also come true, so Lady Macbeth's words make Duncan believe that he has really come to a hermits' dwelling.

iii.   *How does Duncan image Macbeth's love? What is the significance of this image?*

Ans.: A spur is used when the rider wants to quicken his horse's speed. Duncan compares Macbeth's love to a spur that has enabled him to reach Inverness before the king.

This remark is charged with irony. It is not love that has spurred Macbeth on to reach his castle before Duncan but apprehension. He knows his wife is a strong woman and fears her taking the opportunity presented to realise their ambitions herself. Duncan's innocent faith in his general makes the remark ironical.

iv.   *What makes Duncan's use of the term "purpose" ironical?*

Ans.: The usual custom is that royalty is greeted by the lord and lady of the castle but Duncan had wished to do the reverse. He had meant to be Macbeth's "purveyor", intending to receive Macbeth and give him a royal welcome. But Duncan's "purpose" is defeated because Macbeth has arrived earlier and Lady Macbeth has already made known her "immediate" desire. Duncan's "purpose" of welcome is replaced by the Macbeths' purpose of killing him. This makes the use of the term ironical.

v.   *Write a brief note on the dramatic significance of this scene.*

Ans.: This short scene is filled with dramatic significance as it highlights the theme of appearance versus reality. It opens with the blissful picture of nature that gives the impression of life and growth. The castle has a "pleasant seat" and the martlet has its "procreant cradle" in every nook; the "air is delicate." Everything appears to be in complete harmony. Yet the reality, we know, is that regicide and consequent chaos is waiting in the wings. Lady Macbeth has already declared that Duncan's entrance into her battlements is "fatal" and he will not be able to depart "on the morrow" as he has "purpos'd". Duncan's complete confidence in the generous hospitality of his hosts serves to magnify the horror of the violation of the laws of hospitality that is to follow soon. Thus almost every image and utterance in the scene has an ironical significance in the dramatic action of the play.

Act I, Sc. vii

i. **Multiple Choice Questions**

1. **If it were done when 'tis done... -- Choose the right option to give the meaning of the given quote.**

    a. If there were no consequences to face once the murder was done

    b. If the murder itself guaranteed further complications

    c. If the matter of succession could be settled once the murder was committed

    d. None of the above

2. **If it were done when 'tis done ..... – Choose the correct option to show the relation between the first and the second 'done'.**

    a. consequences; completion

    b. settled; committed

    c. finished; written

    d. none of the above

3. **The phrasal verb 'trammel up' refers to ______________.** **Choose the correct option to complete the sentence.**

    a. fishing

    b. pleading

    c. swimming

    d. praying

4. **Choose the correct alternative that gives a similar image to *violence begets violence*.**

    a. And dash'd the brains out

    b. Their drenched natures lie as in a death

    c. Shall blow the horrid deed in every eye

    d. Bloody instructions, which, being taught, return/To plague the inventor

5. **What does the phrase "bank and shoal of time" refer to?**

    a. the passage of time on earth

    b. boundless ocean of life

    c. afterlife

    d. life on earth

6. **Justice will ensure that Macbeth _____________________.
Choose the right option to complete the sentence.**

    a. is not forced to drink from a poisoned chalice

    b. meets a death as violent as Duncan's

    c. meets death as valiantly as he can

    d. is not treated as a traitor

7. **Through which of the following utterances does Shakespeare portray the retribution waiting for Macbeth were he to kill his king?**

    a. Bloody instructions, which, being taught, return/To plague the inventor.

    b. From this time/ Such I account thy love.

    c. .... His virtues/Will plead like angels, trumpet-tongued...

    d. What beast was't then,/That made you break this enterprise to me?

8. **Which of the following expresses an idea similar to the Indian philosophy of *karma*?**

    a. But in these cases, we still have judgement here ...

    b. Bloody instructions, which, being taught, return/To plague the inventor.

    c. This even-handed justice/Commends the ingredients of our poison'd chalice/To our own lips.

    d. ..... his virtues/Will plead like angels, trumpet-tongued

10. **How does Shakespeare change the notion of pity in this scene?**

    a. Pity is imaged as a powerful figure of heaven's vengeance

    b. Pity is like a fragile new-born babe

    c. Pity is symbolic of Macbeth's moral isolation

    d. Pity is an angelic emotion

11. **"That tears shall drown the wind." – Which of the following options gives the meaning of the clause quoted in the context of the play?**

    a. The storm of protest will be calmed by showers of grief

    b. The winds of change will die down when there are showers of grief

    c. Rain will make the storm more tempestuous

    d. The wind will become fiercer as more rain falls

12. **Macbeth had left the supper table because _______________________. Choose the right option to complete the sentence.**

    a. he felt ashamed to sit before his victim

    b. he was scared Duncan would read his expression of guilt

    c. he felt irritated by the small talk at the table

    d.   he wanted a chance to think alone before committing the act

13.   "Was the hope drunk/Wherein you dress'd yourself?" – Lady Macbeth accuses her husband of having been drunk because ____________________. Choose the correct option to complete the sentence.

    a.   he had given her false hopes

    b.   he was being as useless as a drunkard

    c.   he had a drunken confidence to undertake the regicide

    d.   he had been buoyed by drunken hope

14.   "I dare do all that may become a man;/Who dares do more is none." – What truth is Macbeth expressing in these words?

    a.   That manhood is tied to honour and the one who tries to prove his masculinity through violence 'unmans' himself

    b.   That to be a true man, one should not attempt to do more than possible

    c.   That manhood is more than being ruthless and the one who falls short of ruthlessness is the least of men

    d.   That one is de-humanised when one refuses to do more than one possibly can

15.   Which of the following is evidence of evil lurking in Macbeth?

    a.   I am settled, and bend up/Each corporal agent to this terrible feat.

    b.   What cannot you and I perform upon/The unguarded Duncan?

    c.   Nor time nor place/Did then adhere, and yet you would make both:

    d.   But screw your courage to the sticking-place

16. **Choose the correct option to fill in the blank in accordance to the text –**

    SLEEP : SWINISH : : METTLE : _______________.

    a. METALLIC

    b. UNDAUNTED

    c. ROUGH

    d. UNNERVING

17. **Which of the following is an example of the literacy device of alliteration?**

    a. As we shall make our griefs and clamour roar

    b. He hath honour'd me of late

    c. To prick the sides of my intent

    d. False face must hide what the false heart doth know

18. **The scene is dramatically significant because _______________. Choose the correct option to complete the sentence.**

    a. it shows Macbeth as a free man capable of choosing between good and evil for the last time

    b. it portrays the powerful imagination of Macbeth

    c. it establishes the power Lady Macbeth has over him

    d. it gives Macbeth an opportunity to demonstrate his self-control

19. **How does Lady Macbeth overcome Macbeth's scruples about the murder?**

    a. taunts him about his manhood

    b. mocks his ethics

    c. challenges his love for her

    d. All of the above

20. **How does Shakespeare break the stereotype of women's portrayal in Lady Macbeth?**

    a. Lady Macbeth is a balance of masculinity and femininity

    b. Lady Macbeth is a powerful woman in her own right

    c. Lady Macbeth is as hungry for power as Macbeth

    d. Lady Macbeth is as conflicted as Macbeth

ii. Reference to Context

1. Macbeth: If it were done, when 'tis done, then 'twere well

   It were done quickly: if th'assassination

   Could trammel up the consequence, and catch

   With his surcease success; that but this blow

   Might be the be-all and end-all --- here,

   But here, upon this bank and shoal of time,

   We'd jump the life to come.

   i. *How do these words reflect on Macbeth's current mental state?*

      Ans.: Macbeth has left the royal presence, a breach of etiquette, perhaps feeling suffocated in the benign presence of his benefactor. These words reflect the intensely conflicted state of Macbeth's mind. Even as this point of time, he is undecided at to committing the crime even though he has said earlier "Stars, hide your fires....". He is aware that murder of one who is "here in double trust" is the most heinous of crimes and knows retribution will follow. He keeps circling round the point of consequences because his imagination raises all sorts of hurdles to the act while his ambition spurs him on. He is unable to let go of the temptation and the conflict in his mind is the most telling sign of his moral weakness.

   ii. *Which literary device is found in these words? Explain any one example.*

Ans.: Shakespeare has used the literary device of metaphor in these words. The lines "if th'assassination/ Could trammel up the consequence, and catch/With his surcease success" have the words "trammel", "catch" and "surcease" which signal the metaphorical comparison. A "trammel" is a net for catching partridges or fish while "surcease" is a legal term denoting the stay of proceedings in a suit. Once the birds or the fish are caught, they cannot break free from the net; the trapping ensures the success of the action. Similarly, Macbeth wishes the murder itself to be the net catching the consequences of the crime he would be committing and thus ensure that he will not have to pay the price for it.

iii. *Why does Macbeth repeat the word 'here'? How has he referred to life in this extract?*

Ans.: Macbeth has a very active conscience and the repetition of the word "here" is to emphasise that he is not considering afterlife any more. The repetition expresses his focus being on the temporal world and life on earth.

He has referred to life as "this bank and shoal of time". The imagery gives the picture of a sandbank, that is a narrow strip of land in the vast ocean of eternity. If he could be assured that he would not have to suffer the consequences of his action in this life, he would take the risk and forget about the afterlife.

iv. *How does this soliloquy bear out Lady Macbeth's assessment of Macbeth's character?*

Ans.: Lady Macbeth had said earlier of Macbeth "What thou wouldst highly,/That wouldst thou holily.....". This conveys that Macbeth aspires to status, power and reward but does not wish to get his hands dirty or pay the price for its fulfilment. In this soliloquy, Macbeth conveys the same thought in a different way. He would not hesitate to commit the crime, despite his acknowledgement of its wrongness, if he could be assured that he would not have to bear the consequences. He is afraid not so much of the crime itself but of violating a sacred trust that makes him hesitate. And that is exactly what Lady Macbeth had voiced earlier in her soliloquy in Act 1, Scene 5.

v. *What does the dramatist achieve through this scene?*

Ans.: Shakespeare, through this scene, reaffirms that the Witches had merely kindled Macbeth's own secret desire to obtain the throne. Their words influence him no doubt but do not dictate his course of action. It shows a guilt-ridden Macbeth trying to justify the crime to himself and not totally succeeding till Lady Macbeth taunts him into taking the decision. It is because of this scene that many critics feel that were it not for Lady Macbeth, Macbeth would not have 'done the deed'. However that may be, we must remember the dramatist's ultimate object is to show Macbeth as a tragic hero. This scene shows how Macbeth is torn apart by doubts and then "chastised" by the "valour" of Lady Macbeth's tongue for his vacillation. This scene reinforces the vulnerability of Macbeth and Shakespeare exposes it to elevate Macbeth from a murderous villain to a tragic hero.

2. Macbeth: And Pity, like a naked new-born babe,

   Striding the blast, or heavens' cherubims, hors'd

   Upon the sightless couriers of the air,

   Shall blow the horrid deed in every eye

   That tears shall drown the wind. – I have no spur

   To prick the sides of my intent, but **only**

   Vaulting ambition......

i. *Why does Macbeth feel that Duncan's murder would be a violation?*

Ans.: Duncan was at his castle in "double trust" – Macbeth was "his kinsman and his subject" as well as "his host". In the first case, murdering Duncan was committing regicide which was an unpardonable act of treason. In the second, laws of hospitality dictated that the guest should be protected by the host against dangers, not become dangerous in his own person. Thus in both cases, Duncan's murder would be a violation of the "absolute trust" that Duncan has placed on his "peerless kinsman."

ii. *How does Shakespeare image the reaction to Duncan's murder?*

Ans.: Shakespeare uses a mixed metaphor to image the reaction to Duncan's murder. Duncan's virtues will "plead like angels" and announce the murder to the world. The immediate reaction will be a storm of anger against Macbeth, accompanied by pity for Duncan. The storm will spread far and wide and with such force that will cause a flood of tears for the victim. The storm will be calmed only by this downpour. There is a kind of apocalyptic savagery in the image given by the dramatist.

iii. *Why do you think the metaphor of riding recurs through the play? Which other common Shakespearean metaphor also finds a presence in this play?*

Ans.: The mode of transport over land both in 11th century Scotland and 17th century England was horses. So the riding metaphors not only lend authenticity to the speeches of the Scottish characters but also help the dramatist to establish a connection with his English audience. It also makes the characters relatable to the spectators for riding and horses were common to both.

The other common Shakespearean metaphor found often in this play is the clothing metaphor. Here are two examples – "The Thane of Cawdor lives: why do you dress me/In borrow'd robes" and "Was the hope drunk/Wherein you dress'd yourself?...."

iv. *What is the significance of the word "only" in the extract?*

Ans.: The use of the word "only" is significant in this extract on two counts. It points to the single or solitary reason for the crime and Macbeth's acknowledgement of it. First, its use shows that Macbeth knows it is his own ambition that is the spur (stimulus) to his intent (of being crowned king). Neither the Witches nor Lady Macbeth is responsible, as many critics suggest, for Macbeth's crime. Second, the word "only" also indicates Macbeth's recognition of the insignificance of worldly ambition compared to the spiritual upheaval unleashed in his mind by it.

v. *How does Shakespeare use this scene to his own advantage? Give examples.*

Ans.: Shakespeare uses this scene to portray the facets of Macbeth's character that elevate him from a villain to a hero. Macbeth's response to his wife's tongue-lashing shows him as a husband who does not want to disappoint his wife and makes him a vulnerable man, something that strongly contrasts with his previous image of "Bellona's bridegroom" cutting people open "from the nave to the chops" without compunction. The soliloquy at the beginning of the scene is a powerful example of Macbeth's anguish. It shows him battling his conscience and losing, proving to the audience that he is not yet a slave to his ambition. It also shows him as a man of intellect with a powerful imagination and felicity of speech with visually stimulating images. It portrays Macbeth as an introspective man whose character is certainly not, as some critics have alleged, one of "unmitigated evil." This scene thus makes it impossible to condemn Macbeth as a murderous villain with no thought except his own greed for power. It enables the dramatist to ensure that even Macbeth's later slide into unnecessary violence proves the more tragic.

3. Macbeth: Prithee, peace.

I dare do all that may become a man;

Who dares do more is none.

L. Macbeth.: What beast was't, then,

That made you break this enterprise to me?

When thou durst do it, then you were a man;

And to be more than what you were, you would

Be so much more the man.

i.   *What has occasioned Macbeth's response?*

Ans.: Lady Macbeth has taunted him with irresolution first and then called his love for her into question. She has challenged Macbeth's integrity and accused him of breaking his word by refusing to act when the opportunity has presented itself to get "the ornament of life", i.e. the Scottish crown. Finally, and perhaps the most galling to Macbeth, she has called him a coward for not matching his actions with his deepest desire, comparing him to the proverbial cat who would eat fish but would not wet her feet.

ii. *How is Macbeth's response significant in the course of the play's action?*

Ans.: Macbeth's words convey that he has the courage to do everything so long as it does not violate the natural bonds between man and man. Anyone who seeks to rise above such bonds merely dehumanises himself and therefore sinks lower in the hierarchy. In fact, Macbeth's crimes become increasingly bestial and at the end of the play, his courage is that of a cornered animal – "Bear-like I must fight the course." So, in doing what does not become a man, Macbeth becomes less than a man. This response foreshadows Macbeth's future dehumanisation and raises the central moral issue of the play – what makes man unworthy of being called Man?

iii. *Explain the reference to 'beast' made by Lady Macbeth.*

Ans.: Man occupies the topmost rung in the natural hierarchy because of his intellectual and ethical qualities. Were he to disregard these, he would be denying his nature, thereby becoming "none". Theologically, this means he sinks to the level of animals. Macbeth had already discussed usurpation of the throne earlier, which means he had then been ready to violate the sacred bond of trust between king and subject. His sudden refusal to do so angers Lady Macbeth, prompting her to ask whether he had been an animal when he had discussed the murder with her.

iv. *What is Macbeth's greatest fear voiced in this scene? How does Lady Macbeth overcome it?*

Ans.: Macbeth's greatest fear voiced in this scene is fear of failure which he expresses in his uncertain and anxious "If we should fail?".

Lady Macbeth dismisses his fear with the exclamation "We fail!". This shows her cool determination to overcome her husband's moral scruples and override his objections. Such is her confidence that she refuses to entertain even the thought of failure. It is her assured confidence in their abilities to pull off the attempt successfully that finally makes Macbeth "settled" to "this terrible feat."

v. *What impression does Lady Macbeth give you in this scene?*

Ans.: Lady Macbeth impresses me in this scene as a woman who is unapologetically ambitious. She is intelligent and knows her husband's psychology very well. She uses this knowledge to prick him exactly where it hurts – she challenges his male ego and courage – and goad him into action. Her keen intellect is also reflected in the logical planning of the murder so as to avoid suspicion. She displays a strength of will and purpose that is conspicuously absent in Macbeth; there is an inflexibility and ruthless determination that is almost masculine in nature. At this point of time, she does seem an evil woman pushing her husband on to the "primrose way", much against his wishes.

Act II, Sc. i

i. **Multiple Choice Questions**

1. **"There's husbandry in heaven...". The word 'husbandry' has been used by Banquo because** ____.
    Choose the right option to complete the sentence.

    a. the sky is starry

    b. Shakespeare wishes to signal a withdrawal of the good

    c. there is a storm brewing

    d. Shakespeare wishes to convey that the heavens are marshalling their resources for the fight between good and evil

2. **"Their candles are all out." – This conveys that the night is** _____________. **Choose the right option to fill in the blank.**

    a. starry

    b. bright

    c. moonless

    d. dark

3. **What reason does Banquo give for his sleeplessness?**

    a. He is plagued by his dreams

    b. He is unsure of Duncan's security

    c. He is afraid of Macbeth

    d. He is nervous about his son's security

4. **Which of the following utterances express Banquo's sense of insecurity?**

    a. "How goes the night, boy?"

    b. "And she goes down at twelve."

    c. "Take thee that too."

    d. "Give me my sword."

5. **How does Banquo express the king's mood to Macbeth?**

    a.   The king has been bountiful to Macbeth

    b.   The king is sleeping in measureless content

    c.   The king has presented a diamond to Lady Macbeth

    d.   None of these

6. **"I think not of them." – Macbeth says these words to Banquo because _________________. Choose the right option to complete the sentence.**

    a.   he wants to prove his innocence afterwards

    b.   he hopes to evade suspicion of being Duncan's murderer

    c.   he has to dismiss his own guilt

    d.   he has to force his mind to concentrate on other things

7. **"If you shall cleave to my consent..." – Which of the following expresses the opposite meaning of the word 'cleave' in the given quote?**

    a.   You must cleave to your principles even when in trouble.

    b.   Cleave to the instructions to avoid accidents!

    c.   Such a blow undoubtedly may cleave the skull in an instant.

    d.   Poison ivy cleaves to the walls of the ancient castle.

8. **Which of the following utterances show Banquo's suspicions of Macbeth?**

    a.   "So I lose none/In seeking to augment it...."

    b.   I dreamt last night of the three weird sisters...

    c.   At your kind'st leisure.

    d.   What, sir, not yet at rest?

9. **Macbeth hallucinates about the dagger because _________________. Choose the right option to complete the sentence.**

    a.   he has had no sleep for a long time

    b.   he is deluded by the idea of kingship

    c.   the thought of murder is oppressive to him

    d.   he is driven by ambition

10. How does Macbeth weigh the worth of his eyes in relation to the other senses?

    a.   His eyes are pronounced foolish by his other senses

    b.   His other senses are proved unreliable by his eyes

    c.   Both a and b

    d.   Only b

11. Banquo is unable to sleep because ________________________. Complete the sentence by choosing the right option.

    a.   he is worried about Macbeth's intentions

    b.   he does not wish to fall prey to sinful dreams

    c.   Fleance cannot be found anywhere

    d.   Fleance needs his constant attention

12. Which of the following is related in the same manner as given in the text –

    PACE : STEALTHY : : ________________ RAVISHING

    a.   STRIDE

    b.   STRUT

    c.   STALK

    d.   SPRINT

ii. Reference to context

1. Banquo: All's well.

    I dreamt last night of the Weird Sisters:

To you they have show'd some truth.

Macbeth: I think not of them:

Yet, when we can entreat an hour to serve,

We would spend it in some words upon that business,

If you would grant the time.

i. *What does Banquo mean by "All's well."? What is the significance of the use of "we" by Macbeth?*

Ans.: Macbeth has just said that he was ill-prepared for Duncan's sudden visit to Inverness and had failed therefore to render the hospitality that the king deserved. Banquo reassures him saying that the king was sleeping in "measureless content" and so Macbeth had no reason to worry.

The "we" used by Macbeth is significant because it shows how unconsciously Macbeth has adopted the royal mode of speaking in the plural. He knows that by the time he and Banquo would have the conversation, he would be the king. So he speaks as if he were already crowned.

ii. *Why do you think Banquo brings up the subject of the weird sisters?*

Ans.: Banquo's eyes are heavy as lead but he strives not to fall asleep because he has dreams of the weird sisters. He is mortally afraid that he might give in to temptation and prays for strength to ward off the "accursed thoughts". Banquo wonders if Macbeth too is being similarly plagued, specially as two of their prophecies have come true. He wants to know if Macbeth is dealing with treacherous thoughts as a result of the fulfilment of the prophecies. He brings up the subject of the sisters to look for guidance from Macbeth.

iii. *How does Macbeth equivocate in his speech?*

Ans.: Macbeth blatantly lies when he says he does not think of them. He then equivocates when he invites

Banquo to discuss "that business" at a time convenient for both. Banquo thinks it is about the weird sisters since he has expressed his anxiety about them and agrees. But the audience realises that Macbeth actually wishes to talk after the assassination of Duncan and the "business" would be about Banquo's position regarding it. This is clear from the offer he makes to Banquo. Therefore, like the witches, Macbeth too shows himself a master at equivocation.

iv. *What offer does Macbeth make to Banquo right after this speech and why? How does Banquo respond?*

Ans.: Macbeth offers Banquo "new honours" if he "cleaves" to Macbeth's counsel. Banquo has confessed to having dreamt of the Weird sisters the previous night. Macbeth takes the opportunity to test the strength of Banquo's loyalty to the king by making this offer. Trying to bribe Banquo to support him once he claims the throne shows Macbeth in very poor light.

Banquo, being witness to how the prophecies of the sisters had held Macbeth "rapt" is immediately on his guard. His response is an unequivocal statement of his allegiance to Duncan. He tells Macbeth that he will be a party to Macbeth's proposal only if it does not stain his honour and leaves his heart free from guilt.

v. *How does this scene make clear the difference between Macbeth and Banquo?*

Ans.: This is the first time that Shakespeare shows Banquo too being affected by the witches and their prophecies. But here the similarity ends. Banquo frankly admits to losing sleep because of them whereas Macbeth denies thinking of them, a denial which the audience knows is patently untrue. This scene also shows a striking difference in the reactions of the two to the witches. Macbeth consciously thinks of them and it is his sub-conscious mind that provides the moral promptings. The situation is reversed with Banquo – he does not think consciously of the witches but "cursed thoughts" trouble his dreams, that we now know reflect our subconscious thoughts. This scene therefore clears Banquo of all suspicion while colouring Macbeth a pathetic liar.

2. Macbeth: Now o'er the one half-world

Nature seems dead, and wicked dreams abuse

The curtain'd sleep: Witchcraft celebrates

Pale Hecate's off'rings; and wither'd Murther

Alarum'd by his sentinel, the wolf,

Whose howl's his watch, thus with his stealthy pace,

With Tarquin's ravishing strides, towards his design

Moves like a ghost.

i. *What is the mood created by Macbeth's words in this soliloquy?*

Ans.: The soliloquy creates a mood of fear and foreboding. Macbeth's vivid imagination creates the ominous atmosphere in which the "bloody business" will occur. The references to the dark hours of the night, witchcraft and Hecate, howling of the wolf signalling the find of a victim for murder, all create a sinister atmosphere that is redolent with the scent and sound of evil. The words cast a hypnotic spell on the audience and convey a sense of helplessness in Macbeth that disarms him in the battle against evil.

ii. *Why does Macbeth allude to Tarquin in this extract?*

Ans.: Tarquin was a son of the last Etruscan king Lucius Tarquinius Superbus. Tarquin had raped his beautiful hostess Lucrece, the wife of his friend Collatinus, in the dead of the night. In doing so, Tarquin broke both the bonds of friendship as well as the bonds that exist between a host and his guest. Duncan has showered love and honours on Macbeth unreservedly and at present, he is Macbeth's guest. Though the situation is reversed here with the host betraying the guest, Macbeth alludes to Tarquin because of the similarity in the element of betrayal at night when one is most susceptible to danger – Duncan is his friend and benefactor and instead of guarding his guest that night, Macbeth the host is himself going to be his murderer.

iii. *What impression does Macbeth's plea at the end of this soliloquy leave on you?*

Ans.: Macbeth's plea at the end of this soliloquy leaves the impression of a fearful man knowingly going to his own damnation. There is no gloating at the thought of the power he would soon be getting or even happiness that soon his ambition will be fulfilled. It is almost as if Macbeth feels himself in a trance that enables him to act as planned and is afraid that the sound of his own footsteps will wake him up and disable him. Macbeth himself is filled with horror at what he is about to do, yet finds himself too infirm to stop himself from doing it. The soliloquy arouses pity, one of the defining features of a tragedy, and gives Macbeth the status of a tragic hero.

iv. *What is the significance of the bell that rings soon after these words?*

Ans.: The bell that rings is like the death knell of not only Duncan but also for Macbeth. It signals to him that the time was right to commit the murder of Duncan. It also signals to the audience that Macbeth will become "none" once he dares to do more than "what may become a man". The bell's ringing thus spells doom for Macbeth.

v. *What skills of Shakespeare are evident in this scene?*

Ans.: This scene is an excellent example of Shakespeare's skilful use of language to build up the atmosphere of suspense and his art of characterisation. The

Shakespearean stage lacked props that help create atmosphere today. It is with such evocative language that Shakespeare created different atmospheres according to need. Here, Shakespeare has to create the sense of the unnatural overwhelming the natural order. And so he makes Macbeth talk about nature being dead, dreams that are wicked, celebrations of witchcraft culminating in the image of murder stealthily but speedily moving towards its target. The words are enough to make one's hair stand on end in fearful anticipation. Secondly, Shakespeare also uses this scene to ennoble Banquo to please his sovereign and patron, King James I of England. Since James claimed lineage from Banquo, he must be cleared of even the smallest stain of doubt. Shakespeare, however, does not make the mistake of making Banquo an ideal character. Banquo is plagued by "accursed thoughts" in his dreams and that makes him relatable as a flesh-and-blood man. It is in his categorical rejection of Macbeth's rather ambiguous offer that highlights his moral fortitude in contrast to Macbeth. Through the dialogues between the two in this scene, Shakespeare not only portrays Banquo as truly noble but also makes the audience realise how ignoble Macbeth had already become since the time the two had met the sisters on the heath.

Act II, Scene ii

i. **Multiple Choice Questions**

   1. **According to Lady Macbeth, what function does the owl perform?**

      a. sentinel

      b. signaller

      c. collector

      d. guardian

2. **Which of the following utterances show that Lady Macbeth has not been filled with the "direst cruelty" by the spirits?**

    a.   I am afraid they have awak'd,/And 'tis not done

    b.   I laid their daggers ready;/He could not miss them

    c.   Had he not resembled/My father as he slept, I had done't

    d.   There are two lodg'd together

3. **Choose the right option to fill in the blank according to text –**

    OWL : SCREAM : : _____________ : CRY

    a.   CRICKETS

    b.   BABIES

    c.   WOLVES

    d.   MARTLETS

4. **Choose the right option to complete the sentence --- Macbeth describes his bloodied hands as a sorry sight because _____________.**

    a.   he regrets killing the drunken grooms

    b.   he grieves for the dead Duncan

    c.   they tell him of his own degradation

    d.   the blood needed to be washed off

5. **Which of the following is an example of foreshadowing as well as irony?**

    a.   ".....so, it will make us mad."

    b.   "This is a sorry sight."

    c.   "Chief nourisher in life's feast –"

    d.   How easy is it then!"

6. **What made Macbeth unable to pronounce "Amen"?**

   a.   He had had too much to drink

   b.   He had lost consciousness

   c.   He felt he had no right to say the word

   d.   He had sinned against God and man

7. **"I am afraid to think what I have done;/Look on't again I dare not." --- Macbeth does not dare to return to Duncan's chamber because _____________________. Complete the sentence with the right option.**

   a.   a. he is afraid of being killed

   b.   he will be blamed as traitor

   c.   he realises the enormity of his crime

   d.   he feels ashamed of himself

8. **Macbeth sees the dagger dripping blood because _________________. Complete the following with the right option.**

   a.   he is delusional

   b.   he is hallucinating

   c.   emotion has strangled logic

   d.   it is the one with which he will kill Duncan

9. **Lady Macbeth accused Macbeth of cowardice because _______________. Choose the right option to complete the sentence.**

   a.   it was his weak point

   b.   he was refusing to murder Duncan

   c.   she wanted to goad him to action

   d.   it would hurt him

10. **"A little water clears us of this deed:" – What does this reveal about Lady Macbeth?**

    a. She is innocent by nature

    b. She has a practical nature

    c. She has none of her husband's doubts

    d. She is cruel by nature

ii. Reference to context

1. Lady Macbeth: That which hath made them drunk hath made me bold

    What hath quench'd them hath given me fire.

    -- Hark! Peace!

    It was the owl that shriek'd, the fatal bellman

    Which gives the stern'st good-night. He is about it.

    The doors are open; and the surfeited grooms

    Do mock their charge with snores: I have drugg'd their possets

    That Death and Nature do contend about them

    Whether they live, or die.

    i. *How has wine been used by Lady Macbeth as revealed in this speech?*

        Ans.: Wine has been used by Lady Macbeth in two contrasting ways in this speech. She has used it to drug the grooms so that in an inebriated state, they fail to do their duty of guarding Duncan. For herself however, she has used it for the opposite effect. She has drunk a peg or two to give herself the courage to bear the strain of the murderous deed. This also reveals again that, despite the condemnation of some critics, Lady Macbeth is not barbaric or cruel by nature. Whatever she has said about being able to kill an infant that has suckled at her breast is obviously a false notion she has about herself.

ii. *Why do you think Lady Macbeth utters the two words "Hark!" and "Peace!"?*

Ans.: Lady Macbeth is filled with nervous tension because she is uncertain whether her husband will actually be able to murder Duncan. The nerves are stretched taut with the fear of discovery and the slightest noise sets her teeth on edge. The shriek of the owl as it flies overhead is enough to set her heart thumping and she says these two words to calm herself. Only when she identifies the bird does she feel reassured. One can almost visualise the hand gesture to her heart as she utters these words and that tells us Shakespeare very cleverly gave a stage direction to the actor too with these words.

iii. *Why does Lady Macbeth call the owl "the fatal bellman"?*

Ans.: "Watchers" at night would mean being awake. If people the phrase "fatal bellman" is a transferred epithet and the owl itself is regarded in European literature as an ill-omen. In the 16th century, it was the custom of the prison watchman to toll the prison bell at midnight to signal the execution of a condemned prisoner on the morrow. The owl's "shriek" here reminds Lady Macbeth of the prison custom. She is aware that Macbeth has gone to murder Duncan and so associates the owl with the fatal bellman.

iv. *What is the significance of Duncan's grooms praying?*

Ans.: The drugged posset they drank had sent Duncan's guards into a disturbed and restless sleep. It is known today that snoring actually indicates a light sleep and as trained guards, at some level of their minds they sense danger nearby and try to break free of the effects of the drug. Unable to do so, they pray to God for help. Their prayers become significant because of the way Macbeth is affected by them. His inability to say "Amen" at the end of their prayers drives home to both Macbeth and the audience that he has forsaken the path of God and therefore will be deprived of his grace from now onwards.

v.   *Shakespeare was quite the psychologist. What references in this scene may be used to prove the given statement right.*

Ans.: This scene portrays the tension in the couple as they go about the crime. The emotional storm in Macbeth is revealed in his anguished speeches – the way "Amen" stuck in his throat, his hands seeming "hangman's hands" and his eulogy to sleep, all reveal the thoughts raging in his mind. The way Shakespeare points out the benefits of sleep is uncannily in line with later psychological studies. Sleep nourishes and nurtures the human body and spirit. It takes away the cares and anxieties at the end of a hard day just like death brings all worry to an end. Sleep acts as a balm to the weary spirit just as a bath soothes the exhausted body. Sleep is nature's most powerful restorative and so Shakespeare associates it with the second course, that is the chief course, in meals. It helps to calm the "scorpions in the mind" like medicine reduces the pain of a wound. In today's world full of conflict, the value of sleep is understood by one and all and sleeping pills are the rage as we try to escape for a short while into a blissful unconsciousness.

2.   Lady Macbeth: A little water clears us of this deed:

How easy is it then! Your constancy

Hath left you unattended – (Knock) Hark! More knocking

Get on your nightgown, lest occasion call us

And show us to be watchers. – Be not lost

So poorly in your thoughts.

Macbeth: To know my deed, 'twere best not know myself. (Knock)

Wake Duncan with thy knocking; I would thou could'st!

i.   *How does the first line of the extract contrast with what Macbeth has said earlier? What makes Lady Macbeth say these words?*

Ans.: Macbeth has earlier declared that his bloody hands "will rather multitudinous seas incarnadine/Making the green one red." This is in stark contrast to Lady Macbeth's claim that they just need some water to clear the blood off the hands. While Macbeth is talking figuratively about the consequences of the crime, Lady Macbeth is talking literally of the blood staining his hands.

Macbeth's fixation on his hands, a "hangman's hands" as he calls them, irks Lady Macbeth. She wants him to be more focussed on the present and perhaps also washes the blood off her husband's hands as she says these words in reassurance.

ii.   *What qualities does Lady Macbeth demonstrate in this scene?*

Ans.: Lady Macbeth shows herself to be the more practical of the two and almost adopts a motherly role to protect her distracted husband. She is the one to take the precaution of smearing the grooms with blood and laying the daggers beside them to avoid suspicion. Again, she tries to bolster Macbeth with her own confident actions. She is quick to respond to the sudden knocking with the order to Macbeth to put on his nightgown. She is intelligent enough to realise that if Macbeth was seen dressed otherwise, people would wonder why he had stayed awake through the night.

iii.   *Why does Lady Macbeth not want them to be shown as "watchers"?*

Ans.: If people got the impression because of Macbeth's attire that he had not been to bed, questions would immediately arise regarding the reason. Showing themselves as having been asleep instead of awake would make it easier for them to convince others that they had heard nothing to warn them that Duncan was in danger. Lady Macbeth's mind is working clearly and quickly and she knows that it is of utmost importance to their own safety that they be not seen as "watchers" by those who have come to the castle.

iv.   *What do Macbeth's words reveal about him?*

Ans.: Macbeth's words reveal that he is already bitterly regretful of what he has done. They also reveal his weary despair because he knows that he cannot turn back the clock and so must endure the consequences of his action. He understands that it is futile on his part to wallow in guilt because what has been done cannot be undone. He realises that to be fully conscious of the heinous nature of his deed, he must self-alienate, that is, separate the present Macbeth from the past one. So long as he lives, he must accept that he is no longer a valiant hero but a murderer of his king and kinsman.

v. *How does Shakespeare lay the foundations of Macbeth as a tragic hero in this scene?*

Ans.: Macbeth's career is that of a villain but his character is that of a tragic hero because he constantly expresses what should be instead of what is. Shakespeare's art in lies the way he makes a vile murderer into a tragic hero. A tragic hero must retain the sympathy of the audience and Shakespeare achieves this by making the criminal himself denounce the crime. Macbeth never once condones his crime and is his own fiercest and merciless critic. Throughout this scene, we see Macbeth raving in his agony, staring at his "hangman's hands" with horror, in a trance of despair unable to say "Amen" because he has murdered innocent sleep "that knits up the ravell'd sleave of care.....". This profound consciousness of the enormity of his crime and weary acceptance of whatever lies ahead enables Shakespeare to lay the foundations of Macbeth as a tragic hero.

Act II, Sc. iii

i. **Multiple Choice Questions**

1. **If the Porter is the porter of hell-gate, what does that make Macbeth?**

    a.   Beelzebub

   b.   Devil

   c.   Gorgon

   d.   Satan

2.   **Choose the correct option to fill in the blank according to the text:**

   HELL : DAMNATION : : HEAVEN : _______________.

   a.   SALVATION

   b.   TEMPTATION

   c.   BLISS

   d.   REPOSE

3.   **The farmer is brought into the text because _______________. Complete the sentence by choosing the right option.**

   a.   he represents Macbeth's avariciousness

   b.   farmers are symbols of greed

   c.   Shakespeare wanted to create humour

   d.   the groundlings will relate to him

4.   **Shakespeare introduces the Porter scene in the play because _______________. Choose the right option to complete the sentence.**

   a.   he wanted to heighten the tense atmosphere inside

   b.   he wished to undermine Macbeth's crimes

   c.   it enables him to juxtapose the outside and inner worlds

   d.   it helps him to contrast Macbeth with the porter

5.   **Which of the following is NOT an example of equivocation?**

   a.   Woe,alas!/What, in our house?

b.   O, yet I do repent me of my fury,/That I did kill them.

c.   Who can be wise, amazed, temperate and furious,/Loyal and neutral, in a moment?

d.   Confusion now hath made his masterpiece!

6.   **Which of the following matches the expression "the primrose way to the everlasting bonfire"?**

a.   I believe drink gave thee the lie last night

b.   ... we were carousing till the second cock

c.   Who's there, i'the name of Beelzebub?

d.   ...here you may roast your goose

7.   **What does drink 'NOT' do to a man?**

a.   makes him lecherous

b.   takes away his performance

c.   sets him on

d.   equivocates him into a sleep

8.   **Which of the following is an example of the same literary device as found in "darkness light"?**

a.   silver skin

b.   golden blood

c.   joyful trouble

d.   physics pain

9.   **What literary device is there in -- " 'Twas a rough night."?**

a.   Understatement

b.   Hyperbole

c.   Antithesis

d.   Oxymoron

10. **What is the meaning of "...destroy your sight/With a new Gorgon..."?**

    a. become sightless on seeing an image of a Gorgon

    b. become sightless on seeing the sight of the sleeping Duncan

    c. become blind on seeing the sight of the murdered Duncan

    d. become blind on seeing the sight of the sleeping Duncan

11. **The word "downy" is associated with "sleep" by Macduff. Which of the following may also be associated with the same adjective?**

    a. feathers

    b. leaves

    c. flowers

    d. silk

12. **Which of the following is "death's counterfeit"?**

    a. sorrow

    b. sleep

    c. faint

    d. stupor

13. **"O, by whom?" – What does this response tell you about Malcolm's character?**

    a. He is self-possessed

    b. He is curious

    c. He is careless

    d. He is obnoxious

14. **Which of the following proves Macbeth an equivocator?**

    a. Let's briefly put on manly readiness.....

b.   The expedition my violent love/Outran the pauser, reason.

c.   Had I but died an hour before this chance,/I had lived a blessed time

d.   Twas a rough night.

15.   **"....the near in blood,/The nearer bloody." Donalbain says these words because _______________. Choose the correct option to complete the sentence.**

a.   he is a naïve young man

b.   he knows that Macbeth is guilty

c.   he wants to show off his wit

d.   he is suspicious of Macbeth

ii. Reference to context

1.   Banquo: Too cruel anywhere.

Dear Duff, I prithee, contradict thyself,

And say it is not so.

(Enter Macbeth and Lenox)

Macbeth: Had I but died an hour before this chance

I'd lived a blessed time; for, from this instant,

There's nothing serious in mortality,

All's but toys; renown and grace is dead,

The wine of life is drawn, and the mere lees

Is left this vault to brag of.

i.   *What has prompted Banquo's first comment? How is it indicative of his character?*

Ans.: Lady Macbeth, coming out of her chamber, had enquired about the clamour. On hearing that Duncan had been murdered, her response seems to indicate that she regrets not so much the murder as the fact that it had occurred in "our house", that is in the castle at Inverness. This prompts Banquo to say rather pointedly that the murder was shocking, irrespective of its place of occurrence.

Banquo's response indicates his integrity of character. He makes it very clear that he does not condone murder in any way. This is in contrast to the Macbeths who deliberately take the ignoble path to gain the "golden round."

ii. *How has life changed for Macbeth following Duncan's murder?*

Ans.: This speech by Macbeth expresses his true feeling of despondency and a death-wish at this critical juncture. Life has changed drastically since the moment of Duncan's murder. He has been unable to utter "Amen" because Duncan's death signals death of all virtue. It has shorn life of all meaning and has reduced everything worthwhile to the insignificance of toys. For Macbeth, the murder has sucked out all contentment and joy from his life leaving only the dregs, the burden of sorrow, to be borne by him who is still living under the skies.

iii. *What differences do you notice in the speeches of Banquo and Macbeth?*

Ans.: Banquo's speech is characterised by brevity and firmness. It somehow conveys that he is not as taken aback by the sudden horrific event as Macduff. It is a subtle indication that he is suspicious and prefers being circumspect with his words till he knows more about the details.

Macbeth's words are an expression of the depth of his feelings. He himself, rather ironically, is unaware of the profound meaning behind his words because here he speaks, unconsciously, not of himself but for all men. So the words become prophetic of the condition of man when virtue is murdered and vice gains the upper-hand in the affairs of men. The poetry of the speech contrasts with the matter-of-fact nature of Banquo's speech.

iv. *Identify and explain the figure of speech in the last two lines of this extract.*

Ans.: The figure of speech in the last two lines of the extract is a metaphor. The earth, with the sky overhead as the covering of a vault, has been compared to a wine cellar. Duncan's death signals the death of all joy, that is the "wine of life" and with his death, the cellar or earth has been emptied of wine. Nothing except the pain of disillusionment and the burden of sorrow remains. So the last two lines already convey Macbeth's complete disillusionment with power and fame and fortune.

v. *Do you think Macbeth is equivocating here? Give reasons for your answer.*

Ans.: There is a profound philosophical truth revealed by Macbeth that shows he is_*not* equivocating here. Whenever he has equivocated earlier, Macbeth has spoken in hyperboles – "silver skin laced with golden blood", "a breach in nature", "Who can be wise, amazed, temperate and furious,/Loyal and neutral, in a moment?" etc. The words here reflect the realisation of Macbeth's fear of the consequences which he had expressed earlier. We also know that his conscience has been pricking him throughout about the violation of the sacred and natural order that the murder represents. These words echo the deep despair that now fills his soul. Life for him has truly lost its meaning and the only thing for him to do is bear the burden henceforth as best as he can. There is a weariness in this speech that rings true in context of all that he has said earlier.

2. Macbeth: --- Here lay Duncan,

His silver skin lac'd with his golden blood;

And his gash'd stabs look'd like a breach in nature

For ruin's wasteful entrance: there, the murtherers

Steep'd in the colours of their trade, their daggers

Unmannerly breech'd with gore. Who could refrain,

That had a heart to love, and in that heart

Courage, to make's love known?

Lady Macbeth: Help me hence, ho!

i. *To whom is Macbeth saying these words and why?*

Ans: Macbeth is saying these words to Macduff. Macbeth has earlier expressed his regret for killing Duncan's guards in a fit of fury. Macduff naturally is sceptical of this and asks Macbeth why he had acted in such a manner since they had been perhaps the only eye-witnesses to the crime. In response Macbeth tells Macduff that reason was overtaken by the overpowering emotion of a "violent love" at the sight of the dead king and he lost his self-control. These words make Macbeth an equivocator because we know it was his fear of being identified by them that led him to take their lives.

ii. *What does this extract reveal about Macbeth?*

Ans.: This extract reveals that Macbeth can equivocate very well. His description of Duncan's wounds being "like a breach in nature" elevates Duncan from the world of men to the world of nature and reflects Macbeth's own guilt at having violated nature's laws in killing Duncan. Yet we know that his rhetorical question about his inability to stop a loving and courageous heart from avenging the king's murder is patently false. Thus this extract reveals Macbeth's ability to use language as an artifice for dissimulation and that he uses speech as a tool to get him out of a difficult situation. His powerful rhetoric has the effect of silencing the doubts, at least for the time being.

iii. *Do you think Lady Macbeth's faint is real or a pretence? Give reasons for your answer.*

Ans.: Lady Macbeth's faint is a pretence because she is already aware of Duncan's murder. She realises that the others may think that Macbeth was being too eloquent about his love for the king. She fears that in his nervousness, he would let slip something that would arouse the suspicions of the others. She decides to stop him quickly but in a way that would be taken as natural. Fainting was the easiest way and most natural way in the circumstance. It would not only stop Macbeth talking but also divert everyone's attention from Macbeth to her needs. It could also mean that hearing the description, Lady Macbeth realises for the first time the nature of their crime and faints because she is unable to bear the burden of realisation.

iv.   *How is Duncan given a sense of divinity in this speech?*

Ans.: Duncan's dead body is described by Macbeth in language that places him above mere mortality. The expression "silver skin laced with his golden blood" reminds one of the earlier expression "Lord's anointed temple" that Macduff utters when referring to Duncan. Since kings were believed to be God's representatives on earth, the sense of divinity is implied in Macbeth's words. The words give the impression of an ornate painting of a divine figure lying in state.

v.   *Write briefly on Shakespeare's use of imagery in this extract.*

Ans.: This extract has imagery that is almost ostentatious and grandiose. His description of Duncan as he lay dead almost turns him almost into a saintly relic waiting to be worshipped by everyone. Further, Duncan with his body stabbed in various places is metaphorically compared to a decrepit building which has fallen into ruin. The daggers of the grooms, whom Macbeth calls murderers, are also metaphorically compared. Instead of the sheaths that act as their breeches, they are now sheathed in blood. The last sentence of the extract is a rhetorical question which implies that Macbeth's love for Duncan was such that it compelled him to act in the way he did, that is, kill the grooms. Macbeth's imagery highlights, rather ironically, the magnitude of the violation that he is guilty of. Shakespeare reminds his audience that regicide is both unnatural and unholy by his use of imagery in this extract.

3. Malcolm *(Aside to Donalbain)*: Why do we hold our tongues,

That most may claim this argument for ours?

Donalbain *(Aside to Malcolm)*: What should be spoken

Here, where our fate, hid in an augur-hole

May rush and seize us? Let's away

Our tears are not yet brewed.

i. *What makes Malcolm make the opening remark in this extract?*

Ans.: By the time Malcolm and Donalbain reach the scene, Macduff, Macbeth, Banquo, and Lennox are already present and so is Lady Macbeth. There are many exchanges between the thanes and both the sons of Duncan feel themselves side-lined. Malcolm in fact feels that the others were too vociferous of their grief to be really believed. He wonders why they, who are the most affected are not being asked anything about their feelings.

ii. *How does Donalbain convey the current position of the two brothers?*

Ans.: Donalbain conveys the threat to the brothers' lives and their sense of great insecurity very aptly. He does not wish to discuss anything at this moment for fear of being overheard by their enemy who has killed their father. He uses the imagery of death lurking in the tiniest of holes waiting for the right opportunity to strike; Duncan's murderer is unknown and may be as difficult to spot as a tiny hole in the wall. He warns his brother that there may be a plot to kill them too and the best way to save themselves was to flee from the place where their father had met his death.

iii. *Identify the literary device used in "Our tears are not yet brew'd" and explain.*

Ans.: The literary device used here is a metaphor. Tea leaves must be left soaked in boiling water for a certain amount of time for a refreshing cup of tea. Similarly, grief must be given a certain amount of time before it is expressed through tears. Donalbain is explaining to the audience that they must not be shocked to see the brothers dry-eyed in their moment of greatest grief. It is because they have not yet been able to absorb the shock that their grief is not being expressed through tears.

iv. *Why do the brothers decide to "steal away" at the end of the scene?*

Ans.: Like Donalbain, Malcolm is suspicious of Macbeth and not able to trust any of the other nobles completely. Telling somebody of their departure would involve unnecessary talk which at this time is tedious to them. Also, it would mean that whoever wants to harm them would be able to track their journey and fleeing would then be an exercise in futility. Having seen the body of his old father with its wounds with blood oozing, Malcolm is certain that the new world that has been born with Duncan's death will show no mercy to him and his brother. So he feels it is judicious to slip away from Inverness without anyone's knowledge.

v. *Would you call the brothers cowards for fleeing? Give reasons to support your answer.*

Ans.: No, the brothers are certainly not cowards for fleeing; rather they make a wise choice. Hearing Macbeth proclaim his love for Duncan with high rhetoric and Macduff bewailing his sovereign's death, the two brothers exchange their views of the situation. It is Donalbain, the younger of the brothers, who proves the more politically astute and practical. A quick escape from the place would ensure not only their own safety but also give them time to deliberate on their future action in a safe place. There is no one whom they may trust in Scotland and they are already suspicious of Macbeth as Donalbain's words "the nearer in blood, the nearer bloody" reveal a little later. It would indeed have been foolish of them to have stayed when there is clear and present danger.

Act III, Scene i

i. **Multiple Choice Questions**

1. **What does the opening speech of Banquo in this scene reveal about him?**

    a.   Banquo is fearful that Macbeth will kill him

    b.   Banquo feels hopeful that Macbeth will reward him

    c.   Banquo wonders if the witches' prophecies will come true in his case as well

    d.   Banquo feels insecure in Macbeth's castle

2. **What "great feast" does Macbeth invite Banquo to?**

    a.   farewell feast

    b.   welcome feast

    c.   royal feast

    d.   coronation feast

3. **Banquo proposes to ride that day till it is time to attend the banquet because _______________. Choose the right option to complete the sentence.**

    a.   he feels safer outside than inside Macbeth's castle

    b.   he wishes to enjoy the country air

    c.   he wants to teach his son how to fight on a horse

    d.   he has nothing else to do

4. **Banquo takes Fleance along with him because _____________________. Choose the correct option to complete the sentence.**

    a.   Fleance is too young to be without a parent to look after him

    b.   Banquo feels unsure of Fleance's security if left alone

    c.   Banquo wants Fleance to hold his armour

    d.   Fleance can assist Banquo if there is an attack

5. **What, according to Macbeth, were the "bloody cousins" doing at this time?**

    a.   spreading lies about their father's murder

    b.   gathering forces to attack Scotland

    c.   killing time till they attain majority

    d.   begging for alms from the other courtiers

6. **Choose the correct option to fill in the blank according to the text –**

    REGICIDE : KING : : PARRICIDE : _____________________.

    a.   CLOSE RELATIVE

    b.   FATHER

    c.   QUEEN

    d.   MINISTER

7. **Choose the correct option to fill in the blank according to the text –**

    ADVICE: ADVISE : : _____________ : COUNSEL

    a.   COUNCIL

    b.   CONSUL

    c.   CONSULT

    d.   COUNCEL

8.   **Who do you think is the "common enemy of man"?**

    a.   ghosts

    b.   witches

    c.   the devil

    d.   the porter of hell-gate

9.   **"The spring, the head, the fountain of your blood/Is stopped;" – Which of the following has the same figure of speech as used in the given expression?**

    a.   Your face, my thane, is as a book where men/May read.....

    b.   My gashes cry for help

    c.   Come, you spirits/ That tend on mortal thoughts

    d.   Grapples you to the heart and love of us

10.   **Macbeth does not wish to use his power to kill Banquo because _______________. Choose the right option to complete the sentence.**

    a.   he does not want to soil his hands with blood now that he is king

    b.   Lady Macbeth has forbidden him to take such action

    c.   he and Banquo have common friends whose support he fears to lose

    d.   he does not have the courage to kill his friend

ii. Reference to context

1.   Macbeth: Sirrah, a word with you. Attend those men our pleasure?

    Attendant: They are, my lord, without the palace gate.

Macbeth: Bring them before us.

[Exit Attendant. Macbeth thinks out loud]

To be thus is nothing,

But to be safely thus. Our fears in Banquo

Stick deep, and in his royalty of nature

Reigns that which would be feared. 'This much he dares,

And to that dauntless temper of his mind,

He hath a wisdom that doth guide his valour

To act in safety. There is none but he

Whose being I do fear; and, under him,

My genius is rebuked as, it is said,

Mark Antony's was by Caesar.

i. *Is Macbeth's fear of Banquo justified? Give reasons.*

Ans. Banquo had heard the witches' prophecy that Macbeth would be King but Banquo's offspring would be kings hereafter. Macbeth is apprehensive of Banquo's silence regarding the matter and is uncertain whether Banquo would act in the same way as he – Banquo would do to him what he has done to Duncan. Macbeth is also fearful that Banquo may tell others about the weird sisters and their prophecies and point the finger of suspicion for Duncan's murder towards Macbeth. Banquo's soliloquy with which the scene opens is an indication that Banquo may be wary of the instruments of darkness but he is not that keen to disregard their prophecies completely. So Macbeth's fears are justified under the circumstances. So long as Banquo lives, he will be unable to lead his life with any degree of certainty and security.

ii. *Why does Shakespeare eulogize Banquo through Macbeth?*

Ans. Banquo, as presented by Holinshed in his *Chronicles of England, Scotland and Ireland*, is undoubtedly Macbeth's accomplice in Duncan's murder. Banquo's soliloquy at the beginning of Act III, Sc I indicates his "hope" for the future though he hides it from Macbeth. Again, his exchange with his son, Fleance before Duncan's murder reveals that "accursed thoughts" had entered his mind during sleep. Shakespeare's patron as well as his sovereign was James I who claimed descent from Banquo. The editor Dover Wilson argues that Shakespeare could not have depicted James I's ancestor as a cowardly time-server who refrains from exposing Macbeth out of his own ambition and so eulogises him through Macbeth himself.

iii. *What do you think is Shakespeare's motive in presenting the contrasting pictures of Banquo?*

Ans. Shakespeare does not think of Banquo as a hero, so he hints clearly at Banquo's weakness through the contrasting pictures. Shakespeare could not have King James' ancestor as yielding to evil and to Shakespeare himself, cloistered virtue is not as glorious as virtue that is tried and tested, that struggles against temptation and finally vanquishes it. The contrasting pictures of Banquo as revealed through his own soliloquy and through Macbeth's words, do not minimize Banquo's glory but exalt it. The less favourable impression of Banquo at the beginning of the scene is balanced by Macbeth's unwilling tribute to his character. It is all the more impressive because it comes from his intended murderer.

iv. *What literary device has Shakespeare used to bring out the contrast between Macbeth and Banquo.*

Ans. The literary device used by Shakespeare is 'allusion'. The use of the word "genius" alludes to the classical belief that everyman is watched over by a guardian angel. Antony is said to have once consulted an Egyptian sooth-sayer who told him that Antony's genius or good angel became 'fearful and timorous' when near Octavius Caesar's (*Antony and Cleoptatra* – "*....but near him thy* angel/Becomes afear, as being overpow'r'd.")*. Similarly, Macbeth feels that his guardian angel would be overcome by Banquo's angel.

v.   *How does this soliloquy reveal Macbeth's present state of mind?*

Ans. This soliloquy reveals that Macbeth is already beginning to realise how sterile his triumph has been. He has the title of the king but it is Banquo who is royally personified. In obtaining the title of king by 'foul' means, he has destroyed the potential royalty in his own nature and defiled his character. He realises he has banished his peace of mind ("Put rancours in the vessel of my peace") and the last and the worst, has damned his immortal soul ("and mine eternal jewel/ Given to the common enemy of man"). And all to make the seed of Banquo kings! The bargain has been a bad one and in anguished fury, he issues fate a challenge to do its worst. And despite everything, we're forced to admire this man's indomitable courage that refuses to surrender even after acknowledging that all is lost.

2.   Macbeth: Now, if you have a station in the file

Not i' the worst rank of manhood, say 't.

And I will put that business in your bosoms,

Whose execution takes your enemy off,

Grapples you to the heart and love of us,

Who wear our health but sickly in his life,

Which, in his death, were perfect.

i.   *Who is Macbeth speaking to? Where and why have they been summoned by Macbeth?*

Ans. Macbeth is speaking to the two men who had been waiting outside.

They are all in the King's palace at Forres since Macbeth is now the king. Macbeth has decided to murder Duncan but he will not do it by his own hand. He will use the men he has called as his mercenaries.

ii. *How did Macbeth manage to persuade the men to follow his orders? What 'file' is he talking about?*

Ans. This is the second meeting of these men with Macbeth. He has earlier informed them that it was Banquo and not himself, as they had initially thought, who had murdered the king. Apparently, Macbeth has also shown them proof about Banquo having conspired with other "instruments" or agents who had in fact carried out his plan. This is the second meeting and Macbeth demands to know if they are so pious as to forgive the one who has made beggars of their offspring to ensure that his children succeed to the throne.

The men reply that they are "men" which Macbeth takes exception to because it puts them on the same level as he. So Macbeth makes a pretentious discourse on the relative values and status of different breeds of dog, equating them to certain types of men. The 'file' here refers to the 'catalogue' that lists the values of the men.

iii. *Bring out the irony in Macbeth's words.*

Ans. Macbeth talks about the hierarchy of men as defined by the values and gifts which nature has bestowed upon man. Certain qualities that men have naturally raise them above dogs and ironically, Macbeth violates the very order he talks about. He implies in this speech that being a "man" is a "station" whereby one should be ready to commit murder to prove that one does not belong to the "worst rank of manhood". It is very evident that Macbeth himself has sunk to the level of the murderers, though he is loathe to classify himself in the same "station in the file" as them.

iv. *What is "that business" and what will be its effect? Why does Macbeth choose others to commit this crime?*

Ans. "That business" refers to the murder of Banquo and Fleance. Macbeth has managed to convince the murderers that Banquo, prompted by the witches' prophecies, had hatched the conspiracy to kill Duncan and put Fleance on the throne. Macbeth has also persuaded them that Banquo is their common enemy because he has deprived the kingdom of its rightful ruler. If both Banquo and Fleance are killed, then their common enemy would be eliminated. Banquo's death would ensure perfect health and happiness for all of them and bind them to Macbeth in greater love and affection.

As King and as prime suspect in Duncan's murder, Macbeth knows that he cannot risk further suspicion. He also knows from his reaction to Duncan's murder that he may lose his nerve at the crucial moment and put himself in jeopardy. So Macbeth chooses others to avoid the possibility of any mishap.

v. *What does this scene reveal about Macbeth?*

Ans. This scene reveals the fast-paced degeneration of Macbeth. He no longer has to be egged on by Lady Macbeth but is taking the burden on his own shoulders. He has planned the murder of a close friend and comrade-in-arms with cold-blooded deliberation. He has ascertained Banquo's movements with casual skill and has insisted on Banquo's presence at the banquet to be held later to avoid even Lady Macbeth's questions. He has already contracted two professionals to carry out the task, persuading them with lies and concocted stories about Banquo. We see "Bellona's bridegroom" even stooping to flattery and falsehood in order to coax and cajole two cutthroats to do his dirty deed. The scene shows that Macbeth has stepped onto the "slippery slope" from which there is no return.

Act III, Sc. ii

i. **Multiple Choice Questions**

1. **Which of the following has the same figure of speech as in "United we stand, divided we fall"?**

   a.   Scarf up the tender eye of pitiful day

   b.   Nought's had, all's spent

   c.   There's comfort yet; they are assailable

   d.   We have scorch'd the snake, not kill'd it

2. **"...what's done is done." – Lady Macbeth says these words to Macbeth because ____________________. Complete the sentence by choosing the right option.**

   a.   she wishes to encourage Macbeth

   b.   she wants to reassure him of their safety

   c.   she wants him to stop brooding over the past

   d.   she wishes to remind him of his present duties

3. **How has the assassination affected the couple?**

   a.   Both are suffering from sleepless nights

   b.   Both are feeling content

   c.   Both are fearful of life

   d.   Both are suspicious of the other

4. **Choose one of the options to fill in the blank according to the text –**

   CLOISTER'D : FLIGHT : : _____________ : JOY

   a.   DOUBTLESS

   b.   DOUBTFUL

   c.   DOUBLE

   d.   DEVILISH

5. **Macbeth does not reveal his plan of murdering Banquo and Fleance to his wife because ____________________. Choose the right option to complete the given sentence.**

   a.   he is uncertain about the success of his plan

b.   he is afraid that Lady Macbeth would not agree with him

c.   he wants to save his wife from further damnation

d.   he wishes to spare Lady Macbeth the burden of more guilt

6.   **What does the expression "Light thickens" convey about the time of the day?**

a.   dusk

b.   dawn

c.   night

d.   morning

7.   **"Come, seeling night...." – What reference is made by the use of the word "seeling"?**

a.   to the practice of sewing up eyes of hawks and falcons to make them manageable

b.   to the practice of stopping up the gaps in the boundary walls

c.   to the use of sealant in leaking pipes

d.   to the use of seals in communication

8.   **Which of the following supports the view that Banquo lies heavy on Lady Macbeth's mind too?**

a.   Gentle my lord, sleek o'er your rugged looks

b.   But in them nature's copy's not eterne

c.   Naught's had, all's spent

d.   Is Banquo gone from court?

9.   **"..... to gain our peace, have sent to peace..." – Choose the option that gives the correct meaning of the quoted line.**

a.   We have banished our peace of mind by not achieving our goal

b.   We have killed Duncan yet not achieved our goal

c.   We have gained peace of mind by sending Duncan to enjoy eternal peace

d.   We given Duncan the peace of death to gain the satisfaction of our own desires

10. **Which of the following show that a distance has grown between Macbeth and his wife?**

    a.   ..... there shall be done/A deed of dreadful note.

    b.   Be innocent of the knowledge, dearest chuck,/Till thou applaud the deed.

    c.   But in them nature's copy's not eterne.

    d.   .... Things without all remedy/Should be without regard:

ii. Reference to context

1.   Lady Macbeth: How now, my lord. Why do you keep alone,

    Of sorriest fancies your companions making,

    Using those thoughts which should indeed have died

    With them they think on? Things without all remedy

    Should be without regard — what's done is done.

    Macbeth: We have scorched the snake, not killed it.

    She'll close and be herself, whilst our poor malice

    Remains in danger of her former tooth.

    i.   *How is Lady Macbeth different from her previous self in this scene? Why does Lady Macbeth chide Macbeth?*

    Ans.: The Lady Macbeth that appears before the audience in this scene is an almost altered personality. There is none of the fire and brimstone that she demonstrated earlier. Instead, there is a fatigue and disillusionment in her words at the beginning of this scene – "Naught's had, all's spent,/Where our desire is got without content....."

    Lady Macbeth chides Macbeth for keeping to himself since he has ascended the Scottish throne. She knows he has been brooding on Duncan's murder and she urges him to stop dwelling fruitlessly on what has been done and cannot be undone.

ii. *What does Macbeth mean when he says that they have only scorched the snake?*

Ans. It is ironical that Macbeth uses the snake imagery to describe this action because it reveals his sub-conscious association with the devil. A wounded snake coils itself up and stings again with greater ferocity. Macbeth compares Duncan's murder to the snake being merely injured and not killed. Therefore, their future as the royal couple is threatened and Macbeth identifies Banquo as the wounded snake waiting for the right moment to bite and kill. So that Fleance could become king. If Banquo and Fleance were to live, Macbeth implies that they may initiate a murderous plot against the Macbeths.

iii. *What does this exchange reveal about the relations between Macbeth and his lady?*

Ans.: It is evident from this exchange that the couple have drifted apart. Lady Macbeth is no longer the dominant partner neither is she his confidante. Macbeth has been sunk in his own thoughts since the murder and has not gone to his lady for mental or spiritual support. Macbeth has isolated himself to such an extent that she too has not had an opportunity to share her feeling of emptiness despite the fact that they have attained their deepest desire. It is quite evident that they are at a crossroads in their relationship and will probably tread separate paths in the future.

iv. *What changes do you notice in their natures?*

Ans. There has been a role reversal – Macbeth has become the moving spirit while Lady Macbeth has become passive. All her fiery energies are used up and she is now weary of life. Remorse and guilt gnaw at her, making her sink into melancholy but the same feelings excite Macbeth into desperate action. Though both feel cheated of the joy they had desired, they deal with it differently. While Lady Macbeth seems to be sinking into depression Macbeth seems to awaken from the trance he had been in before the assassination. The power equation shows a subtle shift with Macbeth becoming bolder and more decisive and cunning and Lady Macbeth becoming a shadow of her former self.

v. *What does Macbeth resolve to do?*

Ans. Macbeth's sense of despair and disillusionment propel him on to carry his revolt against the natural order. He would rather have the universe fall to pieces than suffer from more nightmares. His frustration creates a new mood of desperate ruthlessness and he resolves not to live in such "restless ecstasy" any longer. He plans to kill the snake before it kills him. He tells Lady Macbeth that she must be ready for "a deed of dreadful note" that will soon be done. Macbeth, without the knowledge of Lady Macbeth, has already hired "cutthroats" to murder Banquo and Fleance.

2. Lady Macbeth: What's to be done?

Macbeth: Be innocent of the knowledge, dearest chuck,

Till thou applaud the deed. Come, seeling night,

Scarf up the tender eye of pitiful day;

And with thy bloody and invisible hand

Cancel and tear to pieces that great bond

Which keeps me pale.

i. *What prompts Lady Macbeth's question?*

Ans. Macbeth has just said that his mind is "full of scorpions" because Banquo and Fleance are alive. Lady Macbeth tries to reassure him saying that nature has not made them immortal, so Macbeth should quell the disquiet in his mind. Barely listening to her words,

Macbeth tells her there is comfort in the thought that they are "assailable" and then voices his decision that before the night falls, there would "be done / A deed of dreadful note". This is what fills Lady Macbeth with trepidation and prompts her question.

ii. *What do Macbeth's words to his wife reveal?*

Ans. The exchange between Macbeth and his wife here reveals the changed nature of their relationship. Previously, it had been Lady Macbeth who had bolstered Macbeth with her confidence. Macbeth is aware that like him, she too is disturbed and unhappy. His affection for Lady Macbeth becomes evident as he wishes to spare her further agony and willingly shoulders the responsibility of future actions. Macbeth's words here tell the audience that he feels protective about her and prefers that she remain unaware of his intentions. Macbeth knows that she is now drained of the fire that had inflamed her earlier. He fears that a revelation of his plans for Banquo and Fleance would be perhaps be unbearable for her.

iii. *What keeps Macbeth "pale"? How does he want night to remedy the situation?*

Ans. Macbeth is "pale" with fear and insecurity because of Banquo. He is afraid that Banquo, having seen his reaction to the witches' prophecies, may well suspect Macbeth of Duncan's murder. So long as Banquo lives, Macbeth cannot not rest in peace. Also, Banquo has quite categorically told Macbeth that he is not interested in increasing his honours if that means he may lose his present honours.

He invokes Night to hurry and close with its scarf of darkness the bright and compassionate eye of day, the sun so that the day may not see the nefarious crimes committed by men on the earth. Night will tear up the lease of life that nature has given Banquo and Fleance and thus ensure his own peace.

iv. *What do these words remind you of?*

Ans. These words echo Lady Macbeth's speech before Duncan's murder in Act I, Sc. v. She had invited night to "pall thee in the dunnest smoke of hell/ that my keen knife see not the wound it makes...". Lady Macbeth images night as a shroud made of the thickest smoke raised in hell so that the murderous deed she is about to commit remains invisible. Macbeth invokes night to be so dark as to "seel" all eyes when Banquo's life is taken under the cover of darkness.

v. *What do the last lines of this speech tell you of Macbeth? What do they tell you of Lady Macbeth?*

Ans. The last few lines tell us that Macbeth has come to accept that he's so steeped in evil that there is no scope of return. "Good things of the day begin to droop and drowse" strikes the keynote of the play and since it is not in Macbeth's nature to surrender tamely, he will do everything to ensure that he will end what he has begun, no matter what the cost. The guilty anguish of his mind somehow compels him to step from one crime into another instead of driving him into penitent action. The latter would have been morally right but reduced the scale of tragedy drastically.

Lady Macbeth marvels at Macbeth's words. She is struck speechless by his stern determination. Her silence, rather than being a sign of willing acquiescence, seems more indicative of her weary acceptance of whatever Macbeth decides. Macbeth's words "... go with me" shows that Macbeth is now taking the lead and he expects Lady Macbeth to follow his lead without question.

Act III, Scene iv

i. **Multiple Choice Questions**

1. **What would make the First Murderer "non-pareil"?**

a. Fleance's escape

b.   Fleance's death

c.   Banquo and Fleance's deaths

d.   Banquo's death

2.   **Which of the following does NOT match the given expression -- "cabin'd, cribb'd, confined"?**

a.   humble host

b.   twenty trench'd gashes

c.   ditch he bides

d.   mortal murders

3.   **"But Banquo's safe?" --- What does Macbeth mean here?**

a.   Banquo's death

b.   Banquo's body has been buried

c.   Banquo is secure

d.   Banquo's death is undiscovered

4.   **Which of the following shows that Macbeth is NOT worried about Fleance's escape just yet?**

a.   'Tis better thee without than he within.

b.   Then comes my fit again:

c.   Thou art the non-pareil.

d.   No teeth for the present.

5.   **Macbeth accuses Banquo of unkindness because ________________. Choose the correct option to complete the sentence.**

a.   Banquo is absent from the banquet

b.   Banquo has refused to attend the banquet

c.   Banquo has turned down Macbeth's offer for new honours

d.   Banquo is shaking his bloodied head at Macbeth

6. Macbeth claims to be a "bold" man because __________________. Choose the correct option to complete the sentence.

    a.   he can face ghosts with courage

    b.   he dares to look on a sight that beggars description

    c.   he dares to confront a sight that is more than devilish

    d.   he can commit murder and not complain

7. "....our monuments/Shall be the maws of kites." – What does Macbeth mean here?

    a.   Human graves will become the stomach of kites if the dead refuse to stay buried

    b.   If the dead refuse to stay in their graves, the kites will feed on them

    c.   The stomach of kites will become human graves if the dead rise up from the ground

    d.   None of the above

8. Macbeth is fearful of Banquo's ghost because __________________. Complete the sentence by choosing the correct option.

    a.   it will proclaim him as its and Duncan's murderer

    b.   it will be seen by others and suspicion will resurface

    c.   it will avenge the murders

    d.   he thinks it will become his constant companion

9. What is Lady Macbeth's tone when she utters the words "With most admired disorder"?

    a.   sorrowful

    b.   empathetic

    c.   cynical

    d.   scornful

10. **Which of the following utterances exposes Macbeth's hypocrisy?**

    a. Ourself will mingle with society,/And play the humble host.

    b. There's blood on thy face.

    c. Which of you have done this?

    d. Here had we now our country's honour roof'd/Were the graced person of our Banquo present

11. **What serves as sauce to food when one is eating away from home?**

    a. greetings of the host

    b. ceremonies of the feast

    c. presence of the hostess

    d. spices served at the feast

12. **How does Macbeth console himself at the end of the scene?**

    a. The lack of control was due to guilt which he will overcome soon

    b. The more experience he gains in such villainy, the better he will be at self-control

    c. The lack of experience had resulted in his strange fit of madness

    d. All of the above

ii. **Reference to context**

1. Macbeth: There's blood on thy face.

    First Murderer: 'Tis Banquo's then.

    Macbeth: 'Tis better thee without, than he within.

    Is he dispatched?

    First Murderer: My lord, his throat is cut;

That I did for him.

Macbeth: Thou art the best o' the cut-throats;

Yet he's good that did the like for Fleance.

If thou didst it, thou art the nonpareil.

First Murderer: Most royal sir,

Fleance is 'scaped.

Macbeth: Then comes my fit again.

i. *How does the conversation affect the atmosphere of the scene?*

Ans. The First Murderer interrupts the banquet where Macbeth is playing "the humble host". There is an atmosphere of forced gaiety in the room because nobody is quite at ease with Macbeth. Macbeth himself is on tenterhooks, waiting for news of the success or failure of his plan. With the First Murderer's entry, evil manifests itself into the room and the conversation reveals that Macbeth is consciously and willingly bonding with evil. So the tension in the atmosphere is further increased.

ii. *How is the erosion of Macbeth's nobility evident here?*

Ans. The man we were introduced to as "Bellona's bridegroom" and "valour's minion" has completely disappeared. The man who had the capacity to imagine murder as a horrid act that would shake his "single state of man" has gone too. Murder upsets him still but no longer repulses him such that his spirit rises up in revolt. So he is willing to have others dirty their hands to do what he no longer desires to do himself. Not only this, Macbeth has sunk so low that though he is now a king, he uses flattery to please common cutthroats. This is telling of his degeneration.

iii. *What would Fleance's death along with Banquo's have ensured?*

Ans. Macbeth feels that had both died as planned, he would have achieved perfect happiness. He would have been as sound as marble, as firm as rock, as free to move and act according to his wish as the surrounding air. Their deaths, in other words, would have ensured his personal safety and therefore, peace of mind. We know however that Macbeth is deluding himself for, as he himself has said earlier, "Glamis hath murder'd sleep, and therefore Cawdor/Shall sleep no more, Macbeth shall sleep no more." Nothing henceforth will render Macbeth a free man for like Dr. Faustus, he has sold his soul to the devil.

iv. *What is the effect of Fleance's escape on Macbeth? How does Macbeth console himself?*

Ans.: Fleance's escape revives all the doubts and fears in Macbeth and he feels himself "cabin'd, cribb'd, confin'd" by them. The words evoke a bitter frustration that he is again going to be stifled by their strangling hold on him.

Macbeth consoles himself with the thought that Banquo, "the grown serpent" is dead and so poses no threat. Fleance, "the worm" will in the future become venomous but for the present, is very young and so has no poisonous bite.

v. *What is your response to Macbeth in this scene?*

Ans.: This scene fills one with pity for Macbeth as we note how the once formidable warrior is reduced to a shivering wreck of a man once he has associated himself with evil. In the earlier scene when confronted by the spectacle of Duncan's murder in daylight, he had retained his self-control though his speeches may have sounded too rhetorical. In this scene however, faced with the spectre of Banquo, we see his complete mental collapse and it is left to Lady Macbeth to draw together the tattered shreds of their dignity and dismiss the gathering. And yet, at the end of the scene we see him resolute once again. And we cannot help but feel admiration for this man who calls "fate into the list", challenging it to do its worst to him.

2. Macbeth: Why, so, being gone,

I am a man again. Pray you, sit still.

Lady Macbeth: You have displaced the mirth, broke the good meeting,

With most admired disorder.

Macbeth: Can such things be,

And overcome us like a summer's cloud,

Without our special wonder? You make me strange

Even to the disposition that I owe,

When now I think you can behold such sights,

And keep the natural ruby of your cheeks,

When mine is blanched with fear.

i. *How does Macbeth become a "man again"? Who is Macbeth addressing and why?*

Ans. This exchange occurs in the Banquet scene of the play (Act III, Sc iv). Banquo has been murdered and whenever Macbeth expresses a desire for Banquo's presence at the feast, Banquo's Ghost appears before him, as if in response to his wish. He dissolves in terror and only regains his self-control, becomes a man again, when the Ghost disappears at his command.

Macbeth addresses the other lords whom he had invited to the feast to sit because, disturbed by his disjointed utterances and wondering if he were unwell, they had got up to excuse themselves and leave.

ii. *What difference between himself and Lady Macbeth does Macbeth remark upon in this extract? How does this extract show the change in Macbeth?*

Ans. He remarks upon the differences in their reactions which has forced him to revise his own estimate of himself. He had thought himself brave but seeing her unmoved at the sights which appal him, he feels he has misjudged his own courage. He finds her self-possession remarkable.

So far despite his wild fancies and gloomy suspicions, Macbeth has had enough self-control and determination to shake himself free from their shackles and carry on with his objectives, hiding from public sight the bloody means which made them possible. This scene reveals the complete collapse of his mental powers as he shifts helplessly between being a man and being unmanned as he finally loses all consciousness of the presence of the other lords and talks to the ghost as if they were alone.

iii.   *What are the things that Macbeth dares as a man and what unmans him? How does this scene help in defining the true idea of manliness?*

Ans. Macbeth dares to challenge the "rugged Russian bear, the armed rhinoceros or the Hyrcan tiger" to a contest. He is even willing to fight a dual with Banquo should he live again but his firm nerves tremble at the sight of the "horrible shadow". Something as insubstantial as Banquo's ghost unmans him completely.

This scene makes it clear that true manliness is not defined by physical courage. Moral courage to make the right choices and stand by them, no matter the temptation, is what manliness is all about.

iv.   *How does Macbeth's present state bear out the truth of his previous utterances "I dare do all that may become a man;/ Who dares do more, is none"?*

Ans. Man occupies a certain place in the hierarchy of creation. This hierarchy is maintained when man follows the obligations of human beings. By murdering Duncan and later ordering Banquo's murder, Macbeth destroyed the natural order and denied in the process, his own humanity. In daring to do more than is permissible for man, he has sunk below a man and has become 'none' and so even a ghost, an insubstantial shadow is enough to terrify him who was once "Bellona's bridegroom".

v. *What role does Lady Macbeth play in this scene?*

Ans. This scene shows Lady Macbeth playing the role of Macbeth's wife and lending him her full support for the last time in the play. Since she has no inkling of Banquo's murder, she thinks Macbeth's ravings are the result of a mind over-burdened with guilt for the murder of Duncan. She chides him for not paying attention to his guests and during his outbursts of guilt and rage, she takes charge. She assures the guests that it was nothing but a "fit" that Macbeth suffered from and they were to partake of the feast. Her quick responses save the day for Macbeth as the guests finally leave in a hurry hoping that their king will recover soon.

Lady Macbeth, with her regal graciousness and intelligent handling of a dire situation plays the role of Macbeth's gallant saviour in this scene.

Act III, Scene vi

i. **Multiple Choice Questions**

1. **".... men must not walk too late." – What is the tone of this utterance?**

    a. fearful

    b. cautious

    c. ironical

    d. scornful

2. **"Was that not nobly done?" – Which of the following does the question make a reference to?**

    a. Macbeth had expressed much pity but only after Duncan's death

    b. Spreading the rumour that Fleance had fled after killing Banquo was not noble of Macbeth

c. Macbeth's claim that grief and rage made him kill Duncan's grooms

d. Malcolm and Donalbain's killing of their father was too ignoble to believe

3. **Macduff lives in disgrace because ______________________. Choose the right option to complete the sentence.**

a. he left his wife and children in Macbeth's clutches

b. he has appealed for help from the English king

c. he has been defeated by Macbeth's machinations

d. he has refused to attend Macbeth's coronation feast

5. **What is the dramatic significance of this scene?**

a. To show Scotland being tyrannised by Macbeth

b. To portray the English king's urgent need of Scottish help

c. To portray Macduff as a traitor to Macbeth

d. To show the need for God's grace in Scotland

6. **The English king is referred as "the most pious Edward" because ________________. Complete the sentence with the right option.**

a. he was devoted to the service of God

b. he had the power to heal by touch

c. he spent a lot of his time praying for his people

d. he was God's representative on earth

5. **"with Him above/To ratify the work..." – In which sphere is the word "ratify" generally used?**

a. celestial

b. commercial

c. political

    d.   social

8.   **"All which we pine for now..." – In which of the following has "pine" NOT been used as in the given quote?**

    a.   Most people pine for what they cannot have.

    b.   No matter how much you pine, it will stay beyond your reach!

    c.   My father had planted the pine you see there.

    d.   Work hard and don't pine.

9.   **Which of the following has "clogs" been used in a way different from the given "That clogs me with this answer."**

    a.   Plastic clogs the drains and causes waterlogging.

    b.   These clogs are not the right size for you.

    c.   Exhaustion clogs my brain.

    d.   None of these

10.   **Scotland is described as "suffering country" because ________________. Complete the following by choosing the right option.**

    a.   she is besieged by war and civil strife

    b.   she is mourning the loss of her true ruler

    c.   her people are under the yoke of tyranny

    d.   there is no hero to save her from her misery

ii. Reference to context

1.   Lennox: So that, I say,

    He has borne all things well. And I do think

    That had he Duncan's sons under his key —

    As, an't please heaven, he shall not — they should find

    What 'twere to kill a father. So should Fleance –

But peace! For from broad words and 'cause he fail'd

His presence at the tyrant's feast, I hear.....

i. *What does "So that," signify? Who is 'he' and how has he "borne all things well"?*

Ans. Duncan has been murdered and his sons Malcolm and Donalbain have fled Scotland and taken refuge in England and Ireland respectively. The two witnesses – Duncan's grooms – have been killed by Macbeth in virtuous anger. Banquo too has been killed and Fleance, his son has also fled. "So that," therefore signifies that all these events have worked to Macbeth's favour because despite everybody's suspicions, there is no proof to challenge Macbeth.

'He' is Macbeth and he has "borne all things well" by spreading the rumour that the sons have killed their respective fathers. Being guilty of regicide and patricide, they have all fled. Macbeth, being first cousin to Duncan has ascended the throne without dispute in the absence of Duncan's sons. Everything has worked to Macbeth's advantage.

ii. *What difference do you notice in Lennox's tone from that of the earlier scenes? What is the only thing making him happy?*

Ans. Lennox speaks in a bitterly ironic tone in this extract. Though the speech starts with veiled references to Macbeth's guilt in the murders, Lennox now is quite open in his hatred for Macbeth. In the earlier scenes, Lennox had been loquacious and least suspicious.

Lennox is happy that Malcolm and Donalbain have managed to escape from the murderous clutches of Macbeth.

iii. *What was significance of the feast that Lennox is talking about? Why, according to him, was Macduff living in disgrace?*

Ans. Lennox is talking about the banquet Macbeth had arranged for his lords since the coronation at Scone had been a rather hurried affair. Its significance lies in that Macbeth's ravings and conversation with the Banquo's ghost in the presence of all the lords had probably set tongues wagging and suspicion spreading like wildfire through the nobility of Scotland.

Macduff had even before the feast frankly challenged Macbeth's loyalty to Duncan and refused to attend the banquet celebrating Macbeth's succession to the throne. Lennox felt that Macduff was therefore living in disgrace.

iv. *What makes Lennox pray for divine help in this scene?*

Ans.: Lennox's speeches show that Macbeth's guilt is now widely recognised. His tyranny, described by the Lord in terms of two of the basic symbols of the play (sleep and bloody knives) "...we may again / Give to our tables meat, sleep to our nights, / Free from our feasts and banquets bloody knives." has impoverished the body and spirit of the Scots. It is as if the afflictions that plague Macbeth have infected his kingdom. In contrast, the sanctity of the English king is emphasized and both the Lord and Lennox hope for divine aid to free their country from the tyrant.

v. *Which feature of Greek tragedy has Shakespeare put to use in this scene? How far is it effective?*

Ans.: Greek tragedies had the chorus to highlight the passage of time in the course of the play's action. Shakespeare moulds this feature to serve his own dramatic purpose of showing the deterioration of Scotland under Macbeth's rule (the 18 years rule of the real Macbeth is compressed into nine days in the play). Like Act II Sc iv, this is a choric scene and Ross is replaced by Lennox while the Old Man representing the common Scots is replaced by the anonymous Lord representing the Scottish nobles. Knowledge of Macbeth's crime has spread through the nobility and the scene suggests the beginning of the counteraction against Macbeth.

It is very effective because without the grim picture of the sufferings of the Scottish people, it would have been impossible to show how tyrannical Macbeth had become. That in turn would have undermined the tragic effect because the greater the fall, the greater the tragedy.

2.   Lord : Thither Macduff

Is gone to pray the holy king, upon his aid,

To wake Northumberland and warlike Siward,

That, by the help of these — with Him above

To ratify the work — we may again

Give to our tables meat, sleep to our nights,

Free from our feasts and banquets bloody knives,

Do faithful homage and receive free honors —

All which we pine for now: and this report

Hath so exasperate the king that he

Prepares for some attempt of war.

i.   *Where has Macduff gone and why? What does this tell you about him?*

Ans.: Macduff has gone to England to ask the English king, Edward III, to lend him his army to fight Macbeth. He also wants Edward to persuade the powerful ruler of Northumberland, Earl Siward, to join and support Macduff. Macduff hopes that the three together would prove too much even for Macbeth.

This action of Macduff's shows his desperation to free his country from Macbeth's tyrannical rule.

ii.   *Why was the English king called the 'holy King'?*

Ans. The 'holy King' is the 'pious Edward' of England. He was Edward the Confessor, a pious King who has received Duncan's son Malcolm most kindly in his court. He was widely believed to have the divine gift of healing and had been appointed to safeguard the country's health. He also has the 'heavenly gift of prophecy'. Hence he was considered 'holy' in his times.

iii. *Which king is the Lord referring to? What has been the king's reaction and why does he react so?*

Ans. The king referred to by the Lord is Edward III, the English king Macduff has appealed to for help.

Macduff has revealed how the Scottish nobles have less "meat" on their tables and how they are forced to be loyal to Macbeth for fear of execution. Edward's reaction has been to start preparations for war against Scotland. Macduff's narrative of Scotland's misery along with Malcolm seeking shelter in his court for fear of being murdered has angered him against Macbeth.

iv. *What is the significance of this speech?*

Ans. The speech signifies the growing anger among the Scottish nobles because under Macbeth, they have lost "meat" from their tables, spend sleepless nights for fear, are forced to take bribes and pay homage to him to ensure the safety of their families. Coupled with the exchange between Ross and the Old Man in the last scene of Act III, the speech conveys the general loss of peace of mind and contentment and the cloud of suspicion overhanging the kingdom. The afflictions that plague Macbeth seem to have infected his kingdom. The lines portray the order that has been wrecked by the havoc Macbeth has wreaked upon them.

v. *How is this scene a counterpart to the closing scene of the second act of the play?*

Ans.: This scene is a counterpart to the closing scene of the previous act in that both mirror reactions to Macbeth. In the previous scene the conversations between Ross and the Old Man represent the public reaction to Duncan's murder as something dreadful and unnatural, though nobody suspects Macbeth till then. In this scene, the conversation between Lennox and the anonymous Lord represents the attitude of the Scotch nobility towards Macbeth. Here, however, there is a crystallisation of the suspicion against Macbeth and complete agreement that Macbeth is nothing but a tyrant bringing Scotland to ruin.

Act IV, Sc. i

i. **Multiple Choice questions**

1. **What does this scene reveal about the witches?**

    a.   that they are all-powerful

    b.   that they are not all-powerful

    c.   that they are figments of Macbeth's imagination

    d.   that they suffer from ill-treatment

2. **The First Apparition has the power to _____________. Choose the right option to fill in the blank.**

    a.   read the mind

    b.   read palms

    c.   move woods

    d.   move mountains

3. **What does the "armed head" represent?**

    a.   Macduff wearing war helmet

    b.   Macbeth wearing war helmet

    c.   Malcolm wearing war helmet

    d.   Banquo' s ghost in war helmet

4. **Macbeth is shown a bloody child because ________________. Choose the right option to complete the sentence.**

    a.   the powers wanted to remind him of his childlessness

    b.   the apparition wanted to tell him that Banquo's children would be future kings

    c.   the apparition wanted to convey that a child torn from the womb will be his nemesis

    d.   the powers meant to tell Macbeth that a child born in the wild will be his nemesis

5. **"Thy crown does sear mine eye-balls." – Which of the following is NOT the meaning of the line?**

    a.   The crown's glitter blinds the eyes

    b.   The crown's gloss creates a halo round the eyes

    c.   The crown's glitter burns the eyes

    d.   The crown's gloss makes the eyes brighter

6. **Which of the following is similar to "blood-bolter'd Banquo"?**

    a.   Had I three ears, I'd hear thee.

    b.   And an eternal curse fall on you!

    c.   Ditch-deliver'd by a drab,

    d.   Come like shadows, so depart.

7. **How does this scene leave the audience?**

    a.   Fearful trepidation

    b.   Happy anticipation

    c.   Painfully sad

    d.   Sympathetic

8. **"And take a bond with fate:" – What 'bond' is Macbeth talking of here?**

    a.   promise from the witches that he will remain unharmed till Birnam Woods comes to Dunsinane

    b.   promise from the witches that Macduff will never harm him

    c.   pledge that Macduff will die so that Macbeth may live unafraid

    d.   None of the above

9. **What is the most significant point made by the dramatist in this scene?**

    a.   Macbeth seeks out the witches for the first time

    b.   The supernatural has immense power over Macbeth

    c.   Macbeth does not believe the witches

    d.   The supernatural controls human destiny

10. **How does news of Macduff's fleeing to England affect Macbeth?**

    a.   He is sorry that he hadn't attacked Fife and killed Macduff earlier

    b.   He is angry with fate for not siding with him

    c.   He feels happy that Time has prevented him from committing another crime

    d.   He feels secure in Macduff's absence from Scotland

ii. Reference to context

1. Macbeth: Then live, Macduff. What need I fear of thee?

But yet I'll make assurance double sure

And take a bond of fate — thou shalt not live —

That I may tell pale-hearted fear it lies,

And sleep in spite of thunder ---

What is this,

That rises like the issue of a king;

And wears upon his baby brow the round

And top of sovereignty?

    i.   *When does Macbeth speak these lines?*

       Ans. Macbeth speaks these lines in Act IV Sc i of the play. He has sought out the Weird sisters to satisfy his curiosity about his future as King of Scotland. Following his wishes, the Witches show him a three Apparitions, whose words give him false sense of security. These words are spoken when the second Apparition tells Macbeth that "none of women born" can harm him and he can "laugh to scorn/ The power of man".

ii. *How will Macbeth ensure that he can "sleep in spite of thunder"?*

Ans. Macbeth has been plagued by sleeplessness since he has murdered Duncan. There have been "scorpions" in his mind and he is assaulted by his own guilt that thunders through his soul reminding him of the eternal damnation he has invited on himself. Hearing from the Second Apparition that no one of woman born could kill him made him think that he was safe from Macduff. He at first decides to let Macduff live but then changes his mind to ensure that he can rest undisturbed by fearful suspicion.

iii. *How does the Third Apparition reassure Macbeth? Which theme of the play does this scene elaborate on?*

Ans.: The Third Apparition tells Macbeth to be proud and brave-spirited and ignore all threats against him. It reassures him saying that he will remain undefeated till Birnam Wood moves to Dunsinane to attack him. Naturally Macbeth feels secure in this knowledge because trees uprooting themselves and moving to attack is an impossibility.

This scene elaborates on the theme of equivocation that runs through the play. Macbeth is deceived into a false sense of security by the half-truths told by the Apparitions. He acts according to his interpretation of their words and suffers tragically because of it.

iv. *What impression does Macbeth leave on you in this scene?*

Ans.: This scene excites a strong rejection of Macbeth. This is because this scene reveals Macbeth at his worst without any of the redeeming outbursts of conscience that make us feel sympathy for Macbeth earlier. In this scene, we see Macbeth going to the witches to base his future actions on what they say. Though their previous predictions have only brought Macbeth "toil and trouble", he still believes in them enough to voluntarily seek them out. We see a Macbeth who deliberately decides to kill Macduff's wife and children when Macduff escapes him. This is not only cruel but inhuman proving the truth of what Macbeth himself had said earlier "I dare do all that becomes a man/Who dares do more is none." We see here the inhuman Macbeth who repulses us.

v. *How does this scene portray the fusion of the dramatic with the political?*

Ans.: The row of eight kings all similar to Banquo in appearance reflect the truth of the Witches' prophecy that Banquo's descendants would ascend the Scottish throne. The eighth king appears holding a magic crystal in which Macbeth sees the images of many more, some even with "two-fold balls and treble sceptres" signifying the ascendancy of the Stuart line and their rule over England, Scotland and Ireland in the future. So Shakespeare remains true to the dramatic need of his play. Along with it, he manages to flatter his sovereign and patron of the King's Men, which was Shakespeare's own theatre company. James I claimed Banquo as his ancestor and the "two-fold balls" are taken as the orbs held by monarchs, here referring to James' double coronation at Scone (Scotland) and Westminster (England); the sceptres as his reign over England, Scotland and Ireland. So Shakespeare fuses the dramatic with the political very adroitly in this scene.

2. Macbeth (*Aside*): Time, thou anticipat'st my dread exploits:

The flighty purpose ne'er is overtook,

Unless the deed go with it. From this moment,

The very firstlings of my heart shall be

The firstlings of my hand. And even,

To crown my thoughts with acts, be it

Thought and done.

i. *What is the context of this aside?*

Ans.: Macbeth had been inside the cave with the Witches when he had heard the galloping of horses. Calling Lennox inside after the Witches had vanished, he asks who had come by. Lennox delivers the message that two or three riders had come by to convey the news of Macduff having fled to England. Since Macbeth had just decided that Macduff must die, Macbeth thinks that time has prevented him from doing what would have given him security.

ii. *How does Macbeth address time here? What conclusion does he draw here?*

Ans.: Time is personified here as one who foresees what Macbeth intends and thereby prevents him from acting on his intentions.

Macbeth therefore concludes that from this time onwards, he will let no time elapse between thought and action. The moment he thinks of something he will do it immediately so that he is not thwarted again.

iii. *What does Macbeth plan to do?*

Ans.: Macbeth is going to launch a surprise attack on Fife now that Macduff, its thane, is not there to protect it. Not only is he going to capture the castle, he decides to take the lives of Lady Macduff and their children and anyone even remotely connected by blood to Macduff. In other words, he will wipe out the Macduff clan from Scotland.

iv. *What difference do you notice in Macbeth in this scene?*

Ans.: There is a raw desperation in Macbeth here. He knows that he has already damned himself by believing what the witches had said earlier. He no longer cares to save either his reputation or himself. The cruel streak that was apparent in his exploits on the battlefield have now come to the fore in his nature. In fact, it seems that Macbeth wants to deliberately bring the worst on himself as if to compensate for what he has done.

v. *Do you think that Macbeth proves the maxim – character is destiny? Give reasons to support your answer.*

Ans.: Macbeth does prove the maxim that character is destiny. His "vaulting ambition" is his hamartia or the tragic flaw in his character that brings about his downfall. He yearns for the Scottish crown and had discussed the matter with Lady Macbeth too. This yearning becomes an obsession when his prowess in the battlefield and adulation of his countrymen lead to a heightened awareness of his exceptional powers. Merit transforms ambition into a passion that leads him down the "primrose way to everlasting bonfire." He embarks on a bloody career that earns him the names of "Fiend of Scotland" and "hell-kite" amongst others. Without that tragic flaw, he would not be the Macbeth we see in the play and so he is a true example for the given maxim.

Act IV, Sc. ii

i. **Multiple Choice Questions**

1. **Ross appeals to Lady Macduff for patience because _____________. Choose the right option to complete the sentence.**

    a. he knows Macduff will soon send help

    b. she cannot afford loss of self-control in Macduff's absence

    c. he believes Macduff has some wise plan

    d. she is now the leader they look to for direction

2. **Which of the following does Lady Macduff accuse Macduff of?**
   a. treachery
   b. licentiousness
   c. lechery
   d. madness

3. **Choose the right option to fill in the blank given – WREN : OWL : : HENS : ____________**
   a. TIGER
   b. LEOPARD
   c. FOX
   d. WOLF

4. **"Cruel are the times..." – The times are said to be cruel because ____________. Choose the right option to complete the sentence.**
   a. the Scots are fighting a losing battle with the English
   b. men are being labelled traitors without reason
   c. men are being forced into conspiracy
   d. the Scots are leaving their country in hordes

5. **How does Lady Macduff express the situation of her son?**
   a. Despite being an orphan, he is fatherless
   b. He has a father but is without one
   c. He has not been brought up by his father
   d. He has none but a father

6. **"Poor birds they are not set for." – Macduff's son thinks of himself as a poor bird because ____________. Complete the sentence by choosing the right option.**
   a. he has been left fatherless

   b.   he is too small to be of any use

   c.   he fears losing his mother

   d.   he knows he will be spared death

7.   **Which of the following proves that Macduff's son was a clever child?**

   a.   Then you'll buy 'em to sell again

   b.   If he were dead, you'ld weep for him

   c.   Poor birds they are not set for

   d.   Nay, how will you do for a husband?

8.   **"Then you'll buy 'em to sell again." – What does this reveal about the boy?**

   a.   He is a witty fellow

   b.   He is angry with his mother

   c.   He is modest about himself

   d.   He has a poor opinion of his mother

9.   **"Though in your state of honour I am perfect." – The messenger says these words to Lady Macduff because _____________________. Complete the sentence with the correct option.**

   a.   he feels she should know of the danger of being killed

   b.   he knows that Macbeth's spies are yet to reach Fife

   c.   he is certain of Lady Macduff being an honourable lady

   d.   he feels secure in her presence

10.   **Which of the following, according to Lady Macduff, is a characteristic of "this earthly world"?**

   a.   Doing harm is often praised while doing good is always decried

b. Doing good is considered dangerously foolish while doing harm is considered praiseworthy

c. Doing good is never seen as a fine act while doing harm is applauded

d. Doing harm is scarcely praised while doing good is often applauded

ii. Reference to context

1. Lady Macduff: His flight was madness. When our actions do not,

    Our fears do make us traitors.

    Ross: You know not whether it was his wisdom or his fear.

    Lady Macduff: Wisdom? To leave his wife, to leave his babes,

    His mansion and his titles in a place

    From whence he himself does fly? He loves us not.

    He wants the natural touch.....

    i. *Where has Macduff fled and why? Do you think he made the right choice? Give reasons.*

        Ans.: Scotland is groaning under the yoke of Macbeth's tyranny. There is widespread fear and discontentment. Macduff flees to England where he knows that Edward the Confessor has graciously given shelter to Malcolm, Duncan's elder son. He wants to offer his services to Malcolm when the latter marches with the English army against Macbeth.

        It was a difficult choice for Macduff but probably the only one he could make considering the circumstances. The English army was more powerful in numbers as well as might in comparison to what Macduff could have gathered under him to fight Macbeth because some had already deserted and some would be fearful to revolt openly. Among the Scottish thanes, he was now the only one who could perhaps match Macbeth's prowess in the battlefield. He could not move his family to safety for fear of warning Macbeth as to his intention. So there was no alternative for Macduff except to flee, leaving his wife and children behind.

ii.   *What does Lady Macduff accuse her husband of? Do you agree with her? Give reasons.*

Ans.: Lady Macduff accuses Macduff of cowardice and treachery – cowardice because she thinks he fled due to fear and treachery because he betrayed his wife and children and his people by fleeing Fife.

I agree partially with Lady Macduff that Macduff had betrayed his family and his people. Instead of leaving them at the mercy of Macbeth, he should have seen to their safety before leaving. He could also have gathered his own men and rallied the other thanes under him since all were known to be deserting Macbeth. He fails in his duty as a husband and father by prioritising his duty as a citizen. Paradoxically it is for this reason that I cannot call Macduff a coward or a traitor. For a patriot, the country matters more than family and Macduff was willing to pay the price for his beloved country. It is clear that Macbeth had spies everywhere and would have known if Macduff had made arrangements for the safety of his family before leaving. Then Macduff's ultimate plan to rid Scotland of her tyrannous ruler would have been defeated. As a husband and father he was wrong, but not as a true Scot.

iii.   *How does Ross' interpretation of Macduff's behaviour differ from Lady Macduff's?*

Ans.: Ross is not willing to believe that Macduff was a traitor; he tries to excuse his absence as caused by either wisdom or fear rather than treachery. According to him, Macduff is "noble, wise, judicious" and knows best how to deal with the unexpected troubles of the times they face. He says that the turbulent times has made Macduff behave in such an uncharacteristic manner.

iv. *What does Lady Macduff mean by "He wants the natural touch"? How does she justify her opinion?*

Ans.: Lady Macduff says that Macduff had proved himself unnatural by deserting his wife and children and exposing them to such a lustful tyrant as Macbeth. She bitterly accuses him of lacking the natural affections that made a husband and father protect his family from the least danger.

She uses the example of the wren, the smallest of birds. The wren fights to the last to save her babies from the predator the owl. But Macduff, by leaving them behind, had shown himself as unnatural.

v. *What is the atmosphere in the Scottish countryside at this time?*

Ans.: The atmosphere in the Scottish countryside is filled with apprehension and terror. Men are declared traitors at random without proof of treachery. Rumour is rife and suspicion hangs heavy in the air as people hear different things and know not what to believe as true. Like a ship tossing on a violent, tempestuous sea, the Scots are pummelled constantly by doubt and fearful uncertainty regarding their lives. Both the nobility and the ordinary people are yearning for a return to the times when their tables had meat, their nights provided sleep, and there was peace at heart.

Act IV, Sc. iii

i. **Multiple Choice Questions**

1. **Which of the following accuses Macduff of being Macbeth's spy?**

a. 'I am young, but something/You may deserve of him through me'

b. 'A good and virtuous nature may recoil/In an imperial charge'

c.   'Angels are bright still, though the brightest fell'

d.   'Perchance even there where I did find my doubts'

2.   **"Angels are bright still, though the brightest fell." – What is the allusion here?**

a.   Jesus' crucifixion

b.   Lucifer being ousted from heaven

c.   Gabriel coming to earth

d.   Jesus being sentenced by Pilate

3.   **Which of the following makes Malcolm suspect Macduff of being Macbeth's spy?**

a.   'Why in that rawness left you wife and child.....without leave-taking?'

b.   '.... You have loved him well;/He hath not touched you yet.'

c.   'That which you are my thoughts cannot transpose'

d.   None of these

4.   **Malcolm portrays himself as an even more tyrannous king than Macbeth because _______________. Complete the sentence by choosing the right option.**

a.   he is indulging in wish-fulfilment

b.   he wants to test Macduff's loyalty to him

c.   he is trying to dissuade Macduff

d.   he wants to test Macduff's love for his country

5.   **If Macbeth has been a lamb despite his cruelty, Malcolm portrays himself as a ___________ in his voluptuousness. Choose the correct word to fill in the blank to complete the sentence according to the text.**

a.   Vulcan

b.   voluptuary

    c.   vulture

    d.   vulpine

6.   **What does Malcolm convey about himself by putting Macduff to the test?**

    a.   'He is not gullible like his father'

    b.   'He is as suspicious of everything as Macbeth'

    c.   'He does not trust Macduff'

    d.   'He wants to dissuade Macduff from joining him'

7.   **"But I must also feel it as a man" – How does Shakespeare break a stereotype here?**

    a.   Men, being human beings, cannot give way to their emotions

    b.   Men must not cry even though they feel grief

    c.   Men may feel but keep emotions under control

    d.   Men, because they are human, must feel and express their emotions

8.   **"O, I could play the woman with mine eyes/And braggart with my tongue!" – This utterance is gender specific because _______________________. Complete the sentence by choosing the right option.**

    a.   women use their eyes to impress while men use their tongues to boast

    b.   weeping is associated with women while boasting is associated with men

    c.   women cry to express grief and men boast to grieve

    d.   women weep to express grief and men boast to hide their grief

ii. Reference to context

1. Macduff: Let us rather

    Hold fast the mortal sword, and like good men

    Bestride our down-trodd'n birthdom. Each new morn

    New widows howl, new orphans cry, new sorrows

    Strike heaven on the face, that it resounds

    As if it felt with Scotland, and yell'd out

    Like syllable of dolour.

    Malcolm: What I believe I'll wail

    What know believe; and what I can redress,

    As I shall find the time to friend, I will.

    i. *State briefly the context of this conversation.*

        Ans.: Macduff has left Fife and come to England where Malcolm, Duncan's eldest son and designated crown prince of Scotland has taken shelter. Macduff assumes that Malcolm has sought aid from the English king and will be attacking Macbeth soon to regain his throne. He is eager to offer his services to the true heir. Malcolm, however, is wary of Macduff and unwilling to plunge into anything without first ascertaining Macduff's loyalties. Unlike his father, he decides to test Macduff before bestowing his "absolute trust" on him. Malcolm pretends to have surrendered his aspirations for the throne in order to see Macduff's reaction.

    ii. *Why does Macduff refer to Scotland as "down-trodd'n birthdom"?*

        Ans.: Macduff here uses the familiar image of ancient Greece which shows a soldier with drawn sword standing with legs apart over the body of his fallen comrade and challenging their common enemy. For Macduff, Scotland is not only his native country but his comrade struck down by the onslaught of Macbeth's tyranny. Its people are being persecuted and men lose their lives merely on suspicion. The helpless cries of the widows and the orphans rise to the sky and strike the heavens making it feel their grief as they reverberate. Macbeth's oppression has brought Scotland to its knees and completely subjugated its inhabitants.

iii. *What does Malcolm's response tell you about him?*

Ans.: Malcolm's response conveys that he is in fact more judicious than Macduff himself, though he is the younger of the two. Despite not having grey hairs, he has the sagacity to understand that Macduff may have been pressured by Macbeth to convince Malcolm to a battle of Macbeth's choice. He makes it very clear by his response that only words are not enough to make him grieve for Scotland or believe in the trials and tribulations of its inhabitants. He conveys that he has people in Scotland supplying him with information and he will redress true grievances but in his own time. So he is certainly not going to be impetuous and impulsive and fall right into Macbeth's trap. Malcolm displays here, in fact, some of the "king-becoming graces" such as patience, restraint, generosity and foresight.

iv. *Why do you think Malcolm paints himself in black a little later in this scene?*

Ans.: Malcolm does not know whether Macduff is a turncoat and a spy for Macbeth. He has to first be sure of Macduff's loyalty towards him. The only way to do that is to paint himself in such black colours that Macduff would be forced to reject him as the Scottish king. So he claims to have a lecherous nature, an avariciousness beyond compare and with boundless intemperance that makes him a ruler worse than Macbeth. Macduff breaks down at this, bewailing Scotland's fate that her most legitimate heir, by his own confession, is unfit to rule. Macduff's anguished helplessness convinces Malcolm of his devotion to Scotland and himself.

v. *How does Shakespeare portray Malcolm as a person worthy of being a ruler?*

Ans.: Shakespeare uses the test Malcolm puts Macduff through to give a portrait of Malcolm himself. He shows how Malcolm has the "king-becoming graces" like patience, temperance, perseverance, fortitude etc. by the very fact that Malcolm is waiting for the right opportunity to avenge his father's murder and regain the Scottish crown. The fact that he is using the shelter provided by the English king to muster more forces to march against Macbeth proves his sagacity. Though he is very young, he is not gullible like his father and does not bestow his trust even on Macduff without first putting him to the test. So Malcolm's steadfastness of purpose coupled with his other virtues make him worthy of becoming a ruler.

Act V, Sc. i

i. **Multiple Choice Questions**

1. **Lady Macbeth is agitated even in her sleep because _________________. Choose the right option to complete the sentence.**

    a. she has been corrupted by evil

    b. she is over-burdened with guilt

    c. shc has lost her identity

    d. she fears dying in her sleep

2. **The Gentlewoman refuses to report to the Doctor what she has heard Lady Macbeth say while sleep-walking because _________________. Choose the right option to complete the sentence.**

    a. she is afraid of being killed for spreading lies

    b. she has too much respect to spread rumours about her mistress

    c.   she cares deeply about her mistress's welfare

    d.   she bears no grudge against her master and mistress

3.   **Lady Macbeth ordered her chamber to be constantly lighted because __________________. Choose the right option to complete the sentence.**

    a.   darkness reminded her of the night of Duncan's murder

    b.   her eye-sight was failing

    c.   she feared the appearance of ghosts

    d.   darkness meant death to her

4.   **Which of the following sentences matches the use of the underlined word in – "The heart is sorely <u>charged</u>."?**

    a.   He was charged with the additional duty of VIP security.

    b.   The car's battery had not been charged for quite some time.

    c.   The prisoner had been charged with assault and battery.

    d.   I was charged more than a hundred rupees for it.

5.   **"This disease is beyond my practice..." – The Doctor lacks the ability to cure Lady Macbeth's disease because _____________. Choose the correct option to complete the sentence.**

    a.   she was suffering from dementia

    b.   amnesia has no cure

    c.   hallucinations are not a disease of the body

    d.   he is a doctor of medicine

6.   **Which of the following is the same figure of speech as "deaf pillows"?**

    a.   flouncing waters

    b.   whistling kettles

    c.   whirring fans

    d.   gauzy wings

ii. Reference to context

1.   Lady Macbeth: Yet here's a spot. Doctor: Hark! She speaks. I will set down what comes from her, to satisfy my remembrance the more strongly. Lady Macbeth: Out, damned spot! Out, I say! One, two. Why then 'tis time to do't. Hell is murky. Fie, my lord, fie, a soldier and afeard? What need we fear who knows it, when None can call our power to account? Yet who would have thought the old man To have had so much blood in him? Doctor: Do you mark that?

   i.   *Explain the presence of the Doctor in this scene.*

   Ans.: Lady Macbeth's gentlewoman had seen Lady Macbeth sleepwalking since Macbeth had left to answer Malcolm's challenge in the battlefield. She had seen the Lady rise from her bed, put on her night-gown and write something on paper. After reading it, she would seal it and then return to her bed. What had frightened the gentlewoman was that Lady Macbeth did all this "while in a most fast sleep." So she had called the Doctor for advice.

   ii.   *What is Lady Macbeth referring to by the word 'spot'? How is it ironical?*

   Ans.: Lady Macbeth refers to the spatters of Duncan's blood that had spotted her hand when she had gone to "gild" the grooms with the dead king's blood. She imagines a spatter still remaining on her hand.

   Lady Macbeth had earlier chided Macbeth for staring with horror at his blood-stained hands with the words "A little water clears us of this deed". This speech makes clear that Lady Macbeth sees the blood spot on her hand even in sleep and makes futile attempts to rub it out. It is highly ironical that the very blood she had scorned earlier as too petty to be worried about is now plaguing her nights.

iii. *What do you think is the significance of Lady Macbeth's speech?*

Ans.: Lady Macbeth's speech is significant for two reasons. First, it shows the fallacy of Lady Macbeth's belief that no one would "call our power to account" once they became the king and queen; her own guilt becomes her strongest foe. Second, her words are a direct confession of their complicity in Duncan's murder. For the first time, people other than the audience and the Macbeths themselves have proof of the guilty party.

iv. *What does the Doctor's query imply? What response does it get?*

Ans.: The Doctor's query implies that he is beginning to understand the meaning of Lady Macbeth's disjointed speech and it makes him very uneasy. He is an unwilling witness to her ravings and feels they had no right to hear what Lady Macbeth has said here.

The gentlewoman expresses her certainty that Lady Macbeth had revealed secrets that only heaven had the right to know about. She also expresses her deepest sympathy for her lady's burden of guilt -- "I would not have such a heart in my bosom for the dignity of the whole body."

v. *Why do you think this scene is in prose and not in verse?*

Ans: Shakespeare generally uses verse when he wishes to elevate his characters to a level above the ordinary. So his major characters speak in verse while the minor ones use prose. This scene has the Doctor and the Gentlewoman who are minor characters and so they use prose. The sole major character, Lady Macbeth, who could be expected to speak in verse which helps express highly charged emotions, also speaks in prose in this scene. Undoubtedly, this scene is charged with depths of emotion and one would expect a mixture of prose and verse. But being the artist he is, Shakespeare knows that verse is the language of emotion under control. Lady Macbeth's speech reveals a chaotic jumble of emotions, and a complete disintegration of rationality which signals a loss of control. It is appropriate therefore that she utter her disjointed thoughts reflecting her fragmented emotions in prose.

Act V, Sc. ii

i. **Multiple Choice Questions**

1. **"Excite the <u>mortified</u> man." – Which of the following situations can have the same use of the underlined word in the given quote?**

    a. Somebody has embarrassed you deeply

    b. Somebody has complimented you

    c. You have escaped danger

    d. You have been placed in danger

2. **Choose the correct option to fill in the blank according to the text --**

    RANK : NOBILITY : : _______________ : GENTRY

    a. LIST

    b. ROLE

    c. QUEUE

    d. FILE

3. **What image is conveyed by the metaphor in "He cannot buckle his distemper'd cause/Within the belt of rule."?**

    a. A man trying in vain to pass his belt into the trouser hoops

    b. A man trying desperately to fasten his belt over a swollen belly

    c. A man tying his trousers with a belt

    d. A man using his belt as a whip to enforce laws

4. **Which of the following does NOT refer to Macbeth?**

    a. he's mad

    b. valiant fury

    c. sovereign flower

    d. sickly weal

5. **How will the thanes purge their country of its sickness?**

    a. They will put Inverness under siege

    b. They will sacrifice their lives in the battle against Macbeth

    c. They will put Dunsinane under siege

    d. They will water Scotland's soil with their blood

ii. Reference to Context

1. Lennox: For certain, sir, he is not: I have a file

    Of all the gentry: there is Siward's son,

    And many unrough youths that even now

    Protest their first of manhood.

    Mentieth: What does the tyrant?

    Caithness: Great Dunsinane he strongly fortifies

    Some say he's mad.....

    i. *Where are the speakers and what is the subject of their conversation?*

        Ans.: The speakers are in the countryside near Dunsinane where Macbeth is holed up. They are marching towards Birnam Wood where they propose to join the English army led by Malcolm and his allies. The subject of their conversation is Macbeth who is apparently preparing himself to meet the challenge of Malcolm.

    ii. *What information has Mentieth given them at the beginning of the scene? What has he said about "revenges" and "causes"?*

Ans.: Mentieth has given the news about Malcolm's movement with his "uncle Siward and the good Macduff" along with the English army.

Mentieth says that both Malcolm and Macduff burn with the fire of revenge in their hearts for which they have ample motivation or cause. For Malcolm, it is the assassination of his father while for Macduff, it is the murder of his wife and children.

iii. *What can be gauged from Lennox's information? How does Angus speak about Macbeth?*

Ans.: Lennox's information conveys how almost the whole of Scotland had risen up against Macbeth. Even adolescents whose beards were yet to sprout had joined forces with Malcolm to oust Macbeth from the throne. Donalbain, however, has not joined Malcolm so far.

Angus roundly condemns Macbeth and informs about the revolts that are breaking out against him to remind him of his treasonous conduct. Macbeth has sunk to such depths of ignobility that he feels himself a "dwarfish thief" in the very robes he wears – the title of king mocks the inadequacy of the very man who holds it.

iv. *What does Caithness say about Macbeth?*

Ans.: Caithness says that Macbeth has strengthened the fortifications at Dunsinane but it is in vain. Macbeth is so over-burdened with guilt that his mental powers have disintegrated and he now resorts to violence to exert his control over others. However, Macbeth is failing even in this. The disorder in his own mind is identified with the chaos in his kingdom. Macbeth in reality is fighting himself for he is defending himself against the consequences of his own actions.

v. *What impression do you get from the portrait of Macbeth as drawn by the lords?*

Ans.: What we see in the portrait drawn by the lords is the picture of Macbeth as he himself had feared becoming. The "scorpions" in his mind have truly bitten him into a hollow man bereft of all reason and love. He is truly now a man with his back to the wall with no way of retreat. The lords reveal that all Scotland know of his torment but nobody has come forward in his support; those who obey him, do it out of fear, not love or loyalty. This picture of Macbeth arouses pity, an essential emotion in the audience for a tragedy to be successful. Since we know that Macbeth had regretted every step down the path he had chosen, there is a gradual cooling of the anger we feel at his violent actions. This scene leaves us with a sense of regret that the once adulated national hero had degenerated into a "dwarfish thief" whose death was desired for by all.

Act V, Sc. iii

i. **Multiple Choice Questions**

1. **Macbeth dismisses the English as "epicures" because _______________. Complete the sentence by choosing the correct option.**

    a. he feels the English lead a life of luxury

    b. he envies their easy lives

    c. he is proud of the Scots' hard life

    d. he hates their luxurious lifestyle

2. **Which of the following conveys the meaning of the term "cream-faced" in given in the text?**

    a. pale with fear

    b. fair-complexioned

    c. smooth-cheeked

    d. none of these

3. **Macbeth dismisses the thought of his wife's sufferings because ______________. Complete the sentence with the correct option.**

   a.   he does not want to dwell on her sufferings

   b.   he does not want grief to cloud his judgment

   c.   he hates the thought that no one can cure her

   d.   he prefers immediate action to useless thought

4. **The phrase 'fallen into the ___________" conveys the meaning of "being without meaning or use". Choose the right word to fill in the blank to complete the phrase correctly.**

   a.   sear

   b.   seer

   c.   cere

   d.   sere

ii. Reference to Context

1.   Macbeth: I am sick at heart,

     When I behold -- Seyton, I say! – this push

     Will cheer me ever or disseat me now.

     I have liv'd long enough. My way of life

     Is fallen into the sere, the yellow leaf

     And that which should accompany old age

     As honour, love, obedience, troops of friends

     I must not look to have; but in their stead.....

   i.   *What 'push' is Macbeth referring to? Why is it important for him?*

        Ans.: The 'push' Macbeth refers to is the imminent battle between him and the joint forces of England and Scotland led by Malcolm.

Macbeth realizes that the outcome of this battle will be decisive for him – either he will remain the king or he will be killed as a traitor.

ii. *What, according to you, does Macbeth 'behold' that makes him 'sick at heart'?*

Ans.: Macbeth has had reports of thanes deserting him in large numbers. Seeing the state to which he has reduced his people, he feels intense regret at the realization that it is his fault. It is because of his misrule that they are in such distress and fleeing their own country. That he has reduced brave Scotsmen to the status of refugees pains him deeply.

iii. *How does this speech portray a Macbeth different from the one that had instructed Seyton earlier?*

Ans.: Macbeth had told Seyton sometime earlier to send out more riders and scour the countryside to identify and hang those who were fleeing for they feared to stay on in Scotland. This picture of a ruthless tyrant murdering his own people is a sharp contrast to the Macbeth as revealed in this speech. Here, he is conscious of the viciousness of his actions and feels intensely burdened by it. Such is the depth of his feelings that he even wishes for death.

iv. *What contrast does Macbeth present between his desires and his reality in this speech?*

Ans.: Macbeth expresses his heartfelt desire to enjoy a normal old age that is characterized by honour, love and obedience from those younger to him. He wishes he had a host of friends to enliven the days of his old age. The reality, unfortunately, is different for him and he has no illusions. He knows that even if he lives to a ripe old age, his companions will be "deep curses, mouth-honour, breath,/Which the poor heart would fain deny, and dare not."

v. *How does the dramatist reinforce the idea of the tragic hero through this scene?*

Ans.: The Classical definition of a tragic hero is a character with heroic or noble traits but also with a tragic flaw (*hamartia*) that leads to his/her downfall (*hubris*). This scene shows the loss of self-control and firmness that must characterize a leader. Macbeth here is seen as a blustering bully who takes out his ire against his helpless servants. Then he rages against the doctor for not having medicine to cure either Lady Macbeth or Scotland before sinking into a philosophical summation of his own life. This scene epitomizes the depths to which "Bellona's bridegroom" and "valour's minion" has sunk. At the same time, it also shows Macbeth's own realization of the fall from grace into the endless well of damnation which increases his tragedy. It is through the juxtaposition of the earlier and the present Macbeth that Shakespeare reinforces the idea of the tragic hero in this scene.

Act V, Sc. v

i. **Reference to context**

1. Macbeth: She should have died hereafter;

   There would have been a time for such a word.

   Tomorrow, and tomorrow, and tomorrow,

   Creeps in this petty pace from day to day

   To the last syllable of recorded time,

   And all our yesterdays have lighted fools

   The way to dusty death. Out, out, brief candle!

   Life's but a walking shadow......

   i. *What does Macbeth mean in the opening lines of this soliloquy?*

Ans.: Macbeth expresses his wish that Lady Macbeth should have died at a later date. He has no time to grieve over the loss or mourn the death of his "darling chuck" for he is too busy with his preparations for the fight unto death that he knows is waiting for him. He realizes that he will feel her loss only later.

ii. *What is the function of the repetition of 'tomorrow' in this speech?*

Ans.: The repetition of something, however iconic, often reduces its importance because people become used to it. Here, however, it has the opposite effect. The repetition of "Tomorrow" lends significance by foreshadowing Macbeth's final conclusion about life as expressed at the end of this soliloquy. On learning about Lady Macbeth's death, Macbeth searches for life's meaning through the entire temporal universe ("all our yesterdays....to the last syllable of recorded time") and draws the conclusion that life is nothing but emptiness and tedium.

iii. *How does this soliloquy reflect on Macbeth at this point of his life?*

Ans.: The "valiant fury" that we witnessed in Macbeth just a few minutes earlier has completely evaporated. Macbeth is now wrapped in a cloak of misery as he looks back on his own life and sees how he has been a fool for thinking that his actions had some meaning. The loss of his wife causes further dejection and despair as he sees the absurdity of his attempts to defend himself because death is the inevitable end of everyone. The finality of death makes life filled with our actions meaningless.

iv. *How does this scene portray Macbeth?*

Ans.: This scene portrays Macbeth in all his complexity of character. On the one hand we see the profoundly philosophical Macbeth pondering of such issues as life and death and man's relation vis-à-vis both. On the other hand, we also witness a return to the brave Macbeth of earlier times. There are echoes of "Bellona's bridegroom" in his words – "Blow, wind; come, wrack./At least we'll die with harness on our back."

    v.   *Which of Shakespeare's skills is the most apparent in this scene?*

Ans.: Shakespeare's skill in characterization is the most apparent in this scene. He shows the many facets of Macbeth's character and we regain our sympathy for him after hearing how he has become the scourge of Scotland. We hear his regret in the speech "I have almost forgot the taste of fears....." and feel sympathy for him for we know his valiant struggle to suppress those very fears. We hear the sheer burden that life has become in the words "It is a tale....signifying nothing." Just when we think he is defeated, he rouses himself once again to action, unwilling to surrender even knowing that defeat is staring him in the face. It is this grand heroic revival of a soldier that earns our admiration and elevates Macbeth from a villain to a tragic hero.

D. Model Answers for Important Questions

1. What is the significance of the Opening Scene with special reference to *Macbeth*?

Ans.: The action of *Macbeth* bursts into wild life in its opening scene with thunder, lightning, distant sounds of battle and three apparitions speaking in cryptic language. The women, who are not perhaps women because they have beards, have come to the end of their meeting and are discussing the next one. They plan to meet Macbeth on the heath once the "hurly-burly's done/And the battle's lost and won." However, their reason for meeting Macbeth is not revealed and this arouses curiosity as well as sends a shiver down the spine --- what could Macbeth have to do with these weird creatures? The audience's attention is riveted by this extremely short but intensely dramatic scene.

An opening scene sets the mood and atmosphere of the play and with its combination of witches, thunder, lightning, and distant echoes of battle, *Macbeth*'s opening scene draws one immediately into a world filled with discord and supernatural evil. This scene is an excellent example of the dramatic technique of foreshadowing because its atmosphere of evil and foreboding haunts the rest of the play. The witches' words, "thunder, lightning, or in rain" signify not only tempestuous weather but the tempest that awaits Scotland and in Macbeth's soul; "hurly-burly" is more than the immediate rebellion, it presages the hasty turmoil in the play's action; "battle's lost and won" suggests the game of pitch-and-toss that is about to be played between good and evil. The final words of the witches "Fair is foul and foul is fair" strike the keynote of the play – the ambiguity of good and evil. Good and evil depend upon perspective and are thus interchangeable. This creates confusion in morals which is reflected in the play's progress in action. The words signal the subversion of the good that is to come.

The mysteriousness of the witches coupled with the sense of uncanny terror they arouse embody the spirit of the play itself. The scene is its leitmotif and thus enhances the artistic unity of the play.

2. **Discuss the supernatural element in the Shakespearean tragedy *Macbeth*.**

Ans.: The supernatural on stage presents not only a visual spectacle of the imagined 'other world' but also challenges and complicates our view of the human characters. Shakespeare, being a humanist above all, introduces the supernatural element in his plays to explore how the 'self' reacts or responds both to external and internal forces.

The supernatural element in the Shakespearean tragedy *Macbeth* helps to create and define the atmosphere peculiar to this tragedy. It creates a darkness of "fog and filthy air" that broods over the play and plunges us into a world where "Fair is foul, and foul is fair." Shakespeare's ingenious use of the witches, Banquo's ghost and the unnatural phenomena underline the discord in the human world and its terrifying consequence while addressing his political considerations.

It is the "black and midnight hags" who are always accompanied by thunder and rain who evoke the supernatural in the play from its very first scene. The Weird Sisters are never called 'witches' by Shakespeare; it was a term used by critics that became popularly associated with them. The word "weird" can be traced back to "wyrd" or the fates and hence their supernatural nature. Their incantatory and enigmatic language recalls the language of the ancient oracles and their malicious mischief-making reminds us of the satyrs of ancient mythology, both belonging to the supernatural world. Their phantasmal element is heightened by their seeming to "possess more than mortal knowledge" and ability to vanish at will. Their powers are derived from evil spirits and they are mysterious emanations melting as breath in the wind. Their very presence on stage rouses superstitious dread and a sense of foreboding in the audience.

The supernatural malice is also felt to be working in nature itself. "Lamentings" are heard in the air and "strange screams of death" burst from her; Duncan's horses devour each other in a frenzy; dawn brings no light with it; common sights and sounds such as ravens croaking or rooks coming home at sunset take on ominous tones. Such happenings evoke the sense of evil permeating the land and snuffing out the good, covering Scotland with "fog and filthy air".

The most traditional supernatural device in the play is of course Banquo's ghost. Elizabethan audiences were familiar with Senecan 'revenge tragedies' but Shakespeare does not resurrect Duncan as would be expected. Instead, the master chooses to show Banquo's ghost to twist the knife further into Macbeth's soul by its silent presence. The "blood boltered" Banquo is a fearful apparition seen only by Macbeth just when, ironically, he wishes for Banquo's presence. Its ghastly appearance with "twenty-trenched gashes" and "shaking his gory locks" shakes not only Macbeth but the audience as well with fear and horror. Banquo's ghost is not a motif for revenge as in *Hamlet* or *Julius Caesar*; it is a device to highlight Macbeth's inner trauma and so keep the focus on the psyche of the play's protagonist.

What makes the supernatural element indispensable to the play is its contribution not only to the atmosphere but to the action of the play as well. At each step, it is the supernatural that propels the action forward – Macbeth meets the three sisters and his ambition gains wings; he sees Banquo's Ghost and his incoherent speeches are enough to rouse the suppressed suspicion of regicide in the minds of the courtiers; and finally, the prophecies of the sisters drive him onto a path of bloodshed from which return becomes impossible.

Therefore, the supernatural element contributes to the plot, action and the atmosphere of the play. It is placed in close relation to character revelation as well, giving confirmation and distinct form to inward movements already present. However, its influence is not of the compulsive kind for it does not negate Macbeth's responsibility for his actions. It is used as a device by Shakespeare to magnify Macbeth's *hamartia* (fatal flaw) and increase the depth of his tragedy.

3. **Write a brief note on the Weird Sisters and their role in *Macbeth*.**

Ans.: The critic H B Charlton remarks that the witches are the embodied malevolence which bubbles up from nature's earth and hovering between the natural and the supernatural, fuse the two in the dark mystery of man's universe. In their combination of mystic suggestion and realistic detail, they represent the very spirit of tragedy which begins and continues under their evil shadow. The tragedy of *Macbeth* would lose much of its magnificence without its strange atmosphere and the atmosphere would be much diluted without the presence of the Weird Sisters.

They are, to begin with, invested with a certain mystery – they appear accompanied by thunder and lightning on lonely heaths and talk in incantatory and cryptic language. They propose meeting Macbeth later when "the battle's lost and won" and they vanish with the enigmatic and spell-like incantation "Fair is foul and foul is fair/ Hover through the fog and filthy air."

The Weird Sisters are thus mysterious creatures whose next appearance introduces the element of horror as they now have "withered" looks, "choppy fingers", "skinny lips" and wild attire. They look like women, yet are bearded; their intent is malicious mischief creating havoc in men's lives. In one scene, they are no more than "foul hags" and in another they are terrible spectral beings who fill even stoics like Banquo with surprise.

Shakespeare's witches are thus compounded of both 'corporal' and 'phantasmal' elements. They may be the Fates as the word 'weird' is derived from 'wyrd' meaning fate; they may be just women with extraordinary powers ostracised by society and hence full of vulgar spite; they may be elemental beings, too elusive and with something strangely evil about them with their ambiguous utterances.

Their role in the tragedy is to highlight the atmosphere of a world where the moral code has been turned on its head and everything is in a state of flux. They have no direct role in the action of the play, yet their influence is inescapable in all that Macbeth feels and does in the play. They are the "black, midnight hags" whose darkness broods over the play and Macbeth himself never blames the "juggling fiends" for making him step on "the primrose way" to eternal damnation though he rails bitterly against their riddles and half-truths. Vulnerable to their influence because of his "vaunting ambition", the fulfilment of their greeting him as "Thane of Cawdor" sets him on a murderous path from which return were as tedious as moving forward. Advised to be "bloody, bold and secure", he slaughters Macduff's family without compunction. Assured that "none of woman born" could kill him, he takes on the final challenge of Macduff. Even after being told that Macduff had been "torn from the womb" of his mother, he fights valiantly till the last breath. The Weird Sisters, with their combination of the earthly and the unearthly, leave an indelible imprint of the coarse and the sublime in the tragedy.

4. **What is the significance of Act I, Sc. iii of *Macbeth*?**

Ans.: The audience first meets Macbeth in this scene and the real action of the play begins here. The first scene set the atmosphere of the play with the introduction of the witches (tempters) and their utterance "Fair is foul and foul is fair" while the second gave the picture of the "noble Macbeth" fighting like "Bellona's bridegroom" in loyal service to his king and country. This scene is where both the tempters and the tempted first meet and this meeting acts as the fountainhead for the following actions and events of the play. This scene makes it very clear that the witches are merely the "instruments of darkness" and do not, in any way, enchant or put Macbeth under their spell and compel him to do what they will. Macbeth's asides and soliloquys reveal that he is still a free man having the ability to discern between the right and the wrong. There is something already in Macbeth's mind that responds to the witches' greetings. This scene makes evident that Shakespeare believed in the doctrine of "Character is destiny" and the fortunes of men and women depend on the choices they make instead of chance happenings or outside influences.

This scene is also significant in that it reveals the socio-economic structure in Jacobean England. In the first thirty-seven lines of the scene, the witches recount to each other their actions in the recent past. One of the theories (refer: Derrida's Deconstruction Theory) says that the witches are not gender-specific because they represent both men and women who have been ostracised by society; they therefore symbolise the haves-nots of society forced to live in the woods and survive on whatever the forests provide them with. Though petty and vulgar, their actions serve to highlight how the haves treated the have-nots resulting in a vicious cycle of revenge and further alienation.

5. **What is the significance of the Porter Scene (Act II, Sc. iii) in *Macbeth*?**

Ans.: The Porter Scene is often dismissed as an addition made by someone other than Shakespeare. But the references in it make it an integral part of the play for Macbeth's journey is down the "primrose way into everlasting bonfire." The knocking at the end of the previous scene is echoed by the knocking here and the sense of urgency as Lady Macbeth and Macbeth dress themselves to answer the knock is replaced by the leisurely responses of the porter to the knocks on his gate. Though his appearance and drunken speech takes away the grimness of the previous scene, his words emphasise how Inverness has become Hell due to Macbeth's action with Macbeth as the devil. If he is the porter of hell-gate, it follows that Macbeth is Satan himself.

The knocking at the gate breaks the claustrophobic tension of the previous scenes on the one hand and highlights the fiendish world inside the castle on the other. There had been much carousing at the banquet and the Porter to Macbeth's castle is indignant at being roused to duty so earlier. His words in his drunken stupor are a grotesque commentary on the tragic action, dark comedy at its best. The three individuals he fancies he is admitting to hell have all over-reached themselves like Macbeth ("vaulting ambition")—the farmer, hoping to profit by hoarding his grain, is ruined by a plentiful harvest; the equivocator intending to evade not only human but also divine justice (this is a clear reference to the Gunpowder Plot and Father Henry Garnet's defence of lying under oath in court as 'equivocation' a just means in the cause of religion); and the tailor trying the impossible task of stealing cloth while tailoring a French hose that were close fits. Greed, equivocation and cheating are all elements in Macbeth's soul and perhaps they have been personified to make the audience question about the elements present in theirs.

The equivocator is of course the most powerful of these allusions because it points to one of the play's major themes. The play opens with the witches' "Fair is foul and foul is fair" Banquo has already warned that the "instruments of darkness" equivocate. The Porter's banter with Macduff is equally pointed. His bawdy account of the effect of drink on lechery ("it provokes the desire, but it takes away the performance") reminds us of Lady Macbeth's vitriolic comment to Macbeth "Was the hope drunk/Wherein you dressed yourself?"

The Porter's fantasy of hell-gate and Lennox's account of the natural and supernatural disturbances show the significance of Duncan's murder as a violation of the divine order. The Porter's reflections serve a double dramatic purpose – his patter provokes laughter from the groundlings but the more sensitive among the audience of the time perceive its dreadful irony. The Porter sees visions, in his own way, of Beelzebub, Demogorgon and Hell but being free of guilt, the denizens of Hell become comical instead of horrifying. To the modern audience this scene may provide comic relief, but for the Shakespearean audience it was a reminder of Judgement Day.

6. **What is the significance of the Banquet Scene in the play?**

Ans.: The rising action of the plot structure culminates in the climax of the play Macbeth with the murder of Banquo and Fleance in the previous scene. This scene, the fourth scene of the third act of the tragedy, begins the denouement or the falling action and is the turning point of the play. It concludes its first half (concerned with Macbeth's rise to power) by showing him in regal state entertaining his thanes, and initiates the second movement (the counteraction against Macbeth) by providing the occasion for him to betray himself to the court.

Banqueting is a powerful symbol in the play, combining eating, the basic activity for maintenance of life and health, with human fellowship. Macbeth has already been separated from his fellowmen by his guilty thoughts at the banquet he gave for Duncan in his castle at Inverness, and now ironically, it is the murder of Banquo, intended to enable them to eat their meals without fear, precipitates his final alienation from human society. A banquet is also an ordered festivity, symbolizing the harmonious order in the state – the thanes sit according to their ranks and Lady Macbeth reminds him of the importance of formal, courteous hospitality. As Macbeth has disrupted the moral and political order, so he now disrupts the feasting with "most admired disorder" and the banquet which began with a proper regard for precedence concludes with Lady Macbeth's hasty injunction "Stand not upon the order of your going,/ But go at once."

The hinge on which the plot turns is Banquo and his contribution is profoundly ironic. While in life, he failed to expose Macbeth, he fulfils that duty in death. The appearance of Banquo's ghost unmans Macbeth and in violent reaction he makes compromising disclosures in front of the lords. "Fail not our feast" he had urged Banquo with hypocritical hospitality; Banquo does not fail it and Macbeth is caught, ironically, in the unexpected consequences of the trap that he has himself laid.

The scene is also the turning point for the characters. At the start, Lady Macbeth has the more subdued manner that appeared in the previous scene. She is withdrawn but alert to any signs of weakness in her husband and when he is overwhelmed by the appearance of the ghost, she rises superbly to the crisis, offering plausible excuses to the guests and rebuking him into regaining his self-control. When she finally takes control of the situation and dismisses everyone, she still preserves the pretence of social life even though the cause is clearly lost. This is the last time in the play that we see her asserting herself. At the end of the scene, she seems to be exhausted, having strained all her powers to the utmost to protect her husband. Instead of the expected castigation of Macbeth's behaviour, all we hear is a weary consolation "You lack the season of all natures, sleep." Ironically, these words carry as much meaning for her as for Macbeth for they are the last words we hear from her before the sleep-walking scene.

The progress of Macbeth's character is in the opposite direction. This is the last occasion on which he is overcome by guilt; the last time his conscience projects accusing images through his imagination. At the first appearance of the Ghost, he betrays his guilt, feebly protesting that he did not do the actual killing but instead of collapsing into abject self-condemnation as he had done after Duncan's murder, he is now able to brace himself for the horrors he knows he will face. He definitely challenges the unspoken accusation ("Why, what care I!") and henceforth his speeches have a savage recklessness that betrays his increasing unconcern for consequences. When he finally dismisses the ghost and with it, the last outward expression of his conscience, both have become "unreal mockery". He has achieved the hardened cynicism for which he has striven, and can claim, from the narrow standpoint to which he is now reduced. "I am a man again." Physical courage is all that is left of his earlier nobility. He realises that he cannot avoid exposure but it only induces a weary determination to pursue the course he has committed himself to for "returning were as tedious as go o'er." The self-accusations of his conscience are belittled as "self-abuse" and he determines to bludgeon it into insensibility.

His decision to seek out the Witches shows the decisive change that has taken place. He makes no attempt now to conceal from himself the nature of the evil that he is embracing – evil has become his good. From a brave and loyal general to a treacherous murderer and a villainous spy, Macbeth is set well on the path to becoming the hell-hound of the play's conclusion.

7. **Soliloquy is a major weapon in a dramatist's arsenal. Elaborate on Shakespeare's use of soliloquy in the play *Macbeth*.**

Ans.: A soliloquy is effectively employed by the dramatist to reveal the innermost thoughts of the character, to give insight into motives and conflicts in the character, to heighten the tragic effect, and to supply the audience additional information to the dialogues and actions on the stage. The device of the soliloquy is used to masterly effect by Shakespeare in most of his tragedies, especially *Macbeth, Hamlet,* and *King Lear.* The fact that Macbeth, despite turning into a murderous villain, retains our sympathy to the very end is because of Macbeth's soliloquies that reveal to us his tortured anguish even as he progresses in his "bloody career."

Macbeth's first soliloquy ("If it were done when 'tis done....") reveals him wrestling with his conscience as he contemplates the assassination of the meek Duncan who had come to Inverness in "double trust." He dwells more on the after-effects of the crime rather than the crime itself. If the act could "trammel up the consequences" with the performance of the deed itself, he would hazard the life to come despite the possibility of punishment and do the deed. A heightened awareness of sin recoiling on the sinner and of impartial justice insisting on the murderer being paid back in his own coin makes him vacillate. It is only when Lady Macbeth challenges his bravery that he compels himself to overcome his fears and commit himself to the crime. Macbeth's second soliloquy ("Is this a dagger I see before me....") clearly shows his perturbation at the thought of murder. As the critic Grierson has said, "Macbeth's moral agitation is clearly evinced in this scene. The fearless warrior is unmanned by the evocations of a shaken conscience." Macbeth's equating himself with "wither'd murder" and the "ravishing Tarquin" shows his own awareness of his moral degeneration. The soliloquy is said after the deed is done ("Whence is that knocking?.....") and it reveals a mind reeling under the burden of guilt. Remorse weighs heavy and his words reveal a man almost pleading for forgiveness. This unabashed acknowledgement of being a criminal and the surrender to our mercies keep our sympathies engaged with him. Macbeth's soliloquies are used by the dramatist to portray the gradual deterioration of a man who was once Bellona's bridegroom to a hell-hound. Yet because of their soaring poetry, their glimpses into a tortured soul, they make Macbeth a tragic hero whose life is reduced to a tale, full of sound and fury, signifying nothing.

Lady Macbeth's soliloquies too play a revelatory role with regard to the characters of the play's protagonist and herself. She portrays Macbeth as a man "not without ambition" but he is "without the illness (that) should attend it", he "wouldst not play false/And yet wouldst wrongly win" and he is "too full o'th' milk of human kindness." In talking of her husband, Lady Macbeth reveals something of her own character. She exemplifies the force of ambition that overpowers all scruples in self and others. The second soliloquy when she calls on the powers to "unsex" her, she reveals the extent to which her womanly instincts have been to be suppressed. Her words "Naught's had, all's spent" reveal the profound melancholy that has enveloped her being and adds to the pathos of the tragedy. Banquo's soliloquy throws light on his character. He is no way as noble and perfect as he appears to be for he is also guilty of being ambitious. His soliloquy reveals him to be human, subject to human desires and not an embodiment of moral perfection.

The soliloquy thus functions as an effective dramatic instrument for illuminating character and conflict, for accelerating action and evocation of atmosphere. It is a potent means of self-revelation through which an essentially melodramatic story of crime and bloodshed has been raised to the level of one of the world's greatest tragedies.

8. **How does the sleepwalking scene show a Lady Macbeth totally different from the one in earlier scenes of the play?**

Ans.: *Macbeth* is unrivalled for its presentation of powerful scenes and the Sleepwalking Scene is decidedly one of the highlights of the play. The scene makes it clear that Lady Macbeth cannot be dismissed as the fourth Witch of the play or as a fiend as many critics have labelled her.

Throughout the First Act, Lady Macbeth is the very picture of invincible grandeur. She plays the decisive role, is more commanding than her husband whom she impels towards the deed with her passionate courage and impervious will. She chastises him with the "valour of her tongue", countering his faltering will with her relentless determination. Even after her passion dies down, her will remains indomitable. In the Murder scene, when Macbeth dare not return with the daggers, she does so; in the Banquet scene, she again rises to the occasion to shield her husband though the glory of her dream has already faded. Her weariness and disillusion are reflected in her words "Nought's had, all's spent,/Where our desire is got without content." The words reveal the depths of her desolation which, sinking inwards, saps her vitality. Her energy and quick responses in the Banquet scene are the last flickers among the embers of a dying fire and so her complete transformation in the Sleep-walking scene comes as no surprise.

The Lady Macbeth of the Sleep-walking scene is a ghost of her former self, walking in the dead of night haunted by memories. Who would have thought that the embodiment of "ruthless and undaunted ambition" would be reduced to a bundle of nerves, moaning in despair because "All the perfumes of Arabia" will fail to remove the smell of blood from her hands. She who had invoked the powers of darkness to infuse themselves in her now must have light continually by her side; she who had assured Macbeth that "A little water clears us of this deed" is horrified by an imagined "spot" on her hands that no amount of rubbing or washing is able to erase. She sinks into a "solitary despondency" from which there is no return. Her collapse into a shuddering wreck in this scene proves Lady Macbeth to be as feminine and as human as any other woman.

The Lady Macbeth of the sleep-walking scene arouses our deepest pity. Where Macbeth has hardened himself and managed to transform his guilt into rage, her psychological defences have been washed away. We see a shell of the Lady Macbeth we are familiar with and we regret the loss of a courageous and confident woman. It is tragic that such a forceful, magnetic personality as Lady Macbeth is reduced to a shadow of her former self and ends her life by committing suicide.

3

Towards the Finishing Line

MIND MAPPING LADY MACBETH'S CHANGE IN CHARACTER

Initial nature: Quote

Confirmation of impression: Quote

First doubt arises: Quote

Reassertion of initial nature: Quote

Inklings of change: Quote

Maidservant's observation: Quote

Ravings: Quote

Hallucination: Quote

Impression of a diseased mind: Quote

Curtain call of her life: Quote

Your analysis

THEMES IN MACBETH

1: ______________________________

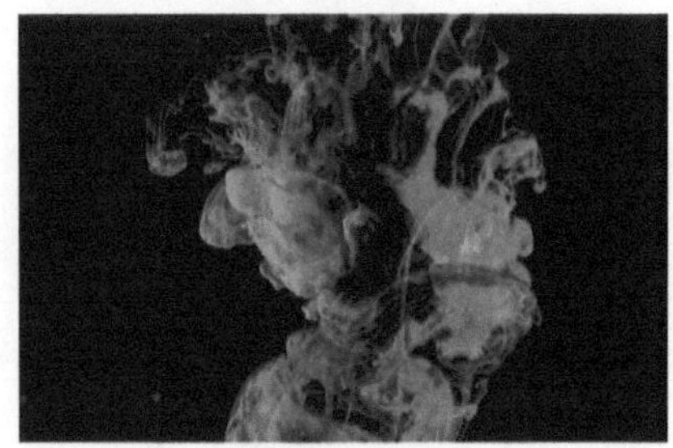

2. ______________________________

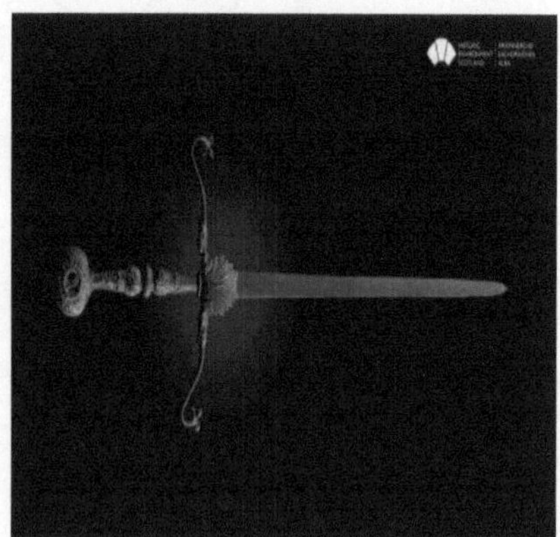

3. ______________________________

4. __________________________________

5. ____________________________

6. ____________________________

THINK AND ANSWER

1. Imagine you are faced with a choice such as Macbeth's to fulfil your dearest ambition. E-mail your friend conveying the situation and your decision.

2. You convey to your friend your decision. He/She tries to dissuade you from your proposed action. Write the conversation voicing your arguments.

3. Do you think Macbeth is an epitome of modern man? Give reasons for your answer.

4. You are Macbeth defending yourself in a court of law. What arguments would you present before the judge and jury to convince them of your innocence?

5. You are Lady Macbeth dissuading Macbeth from Duncan's murder. Write her speech.

6. Malcolm wants asylum in England. As Malcolm, draft an email to the English monarch placing your request.

7. Donalbain does not make an appearance at the end of the play. Why do you think Shakespeare left him out at the end?

8. Corruption in high places leads to oppression of the masses. Write an article on this observation.

4

To Read or Not to Read

ESSAYS BY AUTHOR

1. **Need to include Shakespeare in modern school curriculum.**

   The "upstart crow" of the Elizabethan age rules supreme in Western literature even in the 21st century. It was Ben Jonson who prophetically said of his compatriot "He was not of an age, but for all time!" So what are the reasons that institutions change authors and texts in their syllabi but Shakespeare remains constant?

   Shakespeare illuminates the human experience brilliantly in all its complexity and variety. The vision encompassed in his plays is astonishing. Who can not appreciate the philosophical depth expressed through Prospero "We are such stuff/As dreams are made on; and our little life/Is rounded with a sleep." (*The Tempest*) or "The fault, dear Brutus, is not in our stars,/But in ourselves, that we are underlings." (*Julius Caesar*) or the profundity of "What's done cannot be undone." (*Macbeth*)? Every time we come to a crossroads in life that make us question ourselves, we fall back on Hamlet's words, "To be, or not to be: that is the question:/Whether 'tis nobler in the mind to suffer/The slings and arrows of outrageous fortune,/Or to take arms against a sea of troubles,/And by opposing end them?" Which lover will not want to be wooed by "My bounty is as boundless as the sea,/My love as deep; the more I give to thee,/The more I have, for both are infinite." Like we Bengalies fall back on Rabindranath Tagore to express our feeling with greater accuracy and sensitivity, the English have their Bard-of-Avon.

   Another reason for Shakespeare's continued relevance is the thematic content in Shakespearean plays that transcend not only time but place. We have seen adaptations of *Romeo and Juliet, Macbeth, King Lear* in countries as distant from England as Japan and India. Love, thoughts on fate and free will, death and mortality, ambition and power, betrayal and jealousy, madness and mental illness are some of the themes found in the plays and such themes resound not only in 21st century macrocosm of nations but the microcosms of households.

Marchette Chute gives one reason for Shakespeare's popularity irrespective of spatio-temporal differences in the *Introduction* to her retelling of Shakespeare's stories, "Homer told of adventure and men at war, Sophocles and Tolstoy told of tragedies and of people in trouble, Terence and Mark Twain told comedic stories, Dickens told melodramatic ones, Plutarch told histories and Hans Christian Andersen told fairy tales. But Shakespeare told every kind of story – comedy, tragedy, history, melodrama, adventure, love stories and fairy tales – and each of them so well that they have become the greatest name. (*Stories from Shakespeare*, 11)

The highlight of the dramas is that there is an intermingling of genres in the plays irrespective of the broader category under which they may be classified. Sir John Falstaff is perhaps the greatest comic character but is found in the History plays (*Henry IV Parts 1* and *2*, and *Henry V*); the Fool in *King Lear*, perhaps the greatest tragedy in English literature, is more of a truth-teller than a jester; Feste the wise fool in *Twelfth Night*, a romantic comedy, breaks the barriers between the audience and the characters on stage with his insightful commentary on the play's actors and actions.

Perhaps the most compelling reason is the characters that Shakespeare has delineated in his plays. Not only his audience but also actors are always eager to participate in a Shakespearean play. Shakespeare's tragic heroes like Lear, Hamlet, Macbeth etc. are such sublime creations that they tower even above those of the Greek tragedies. Shakespeare's tragic characters are in fifty shades of grey while his comic ones are part of a rainbow. Even the secondary characters cannot be neglected because they too prove essential to the purpose of the dramatist. They give the actors the opportunity to plumb the depths of their talent in the portrayals and this is an important reason for the enduring appeal of Shakespeare in modern times.

But then again, you may say the appeal of Shakespeare's plays lies in the poetry. When Lear exclaims, "Blow, winds, and crack your cheeks! Rage! Blow!....", we feel all the suppressed anguish of a father who, in his words, is indeed "a very foolish fond old man/Fourscore and upward." This kind of tumultuous speech has its opposite in the speech of another banished father, the Duke in the forest Arden, who says "Sweet are the uses of adversity," and is complimented as one who can "translate the stubbornness of fortune/Into so quiet and so sweet a style." Enobarbus' description of Queen Cleopatra, "The barge she sat in, like a burnish'd throne,/Burned on the water..." is a superb image of majesty painted through words. Perhaps Milton, through his epic similes, is the only one to rival Shakespeare in such picturesque imagery. The poetic "It is a tale/Told by an idiot, full of sound and fury,/Signifying nothing." is an expression of unparalleled Stoicism while "The quality of mercy is not strained;/It droppeth as the gentle rain from heaven/Upon the place beneath." is deeply Christian. There is no end of examples relating to Shakespeare's poetic appeal.

As for me, a person of living in an age torn by "woke culture", "cancel culture", "#metoo", "#lgbtq+", and all the rest, it is his open-mindedness and acceptance of everything that is amazing. He portrays a spectrum of characters, good, bad, ugly, and all shades of grey, but never does he castigate or condemn them. He leaves it to his readers and his audience to interpret them in ways they find comfortable or acceptable. It is this reflection of his non-judgmental attitude that makes the plays relatable to all groups of human beings and helps them to transcend their age and time.

2. **Imagination: An Essential Dramatic Tool in Macbeth.**

Imagination is perhaps the most powerful faculty given to us. It enables us to foresee the future, to go beyond the ordinary, to escape into worlds other than our own, and last but not least in today's fractured world, to empathise. Imagination has empowered scientists to delve into the workings of the universe; it is imagination that has allowed poets to sing of things unknown and writers to enter into the minds of others. Speaking on the ebb and flow of energy during rehearsals, the podcaster and writer for Bell Shakespeare Andy McLean says, "The Macbeths' imagination is what makes the couple great, yet it also destroys them."

Macbeth is a play that cannot be appreciated if one's imagination has been strangled by the ways of the world. The play begins with spirits whose role can only be appreciated if one has imagination; else they may be dismissed as mere demonic creatures with only malicious intent. Their unearthly aura is best realised through the combined imagination of the writer, performer and the audience. Also, their words set alight the pyre of ambition that the Macbeths finally burn on.

And it is the imagination of the audience that the dramatist empowers with his words. We see Macbeth as the all-conquering hero through our imagination before he sets foot on the stage. We hear of Macbeth's and Banquo's exploits on the battlefield and the vivid description helps us to visualise the spectacle in our minds. We hear Lady Macbeth invoke the evil spirits to come and fill her up with direst cruelty from top to toe and we imagine them diffusing themselves in her body and spirit. We do not hear the "lamentings" or the "strange screams of death" reported the night before the night before Duncan's murder but our imaginations make them ring in our ears. We do not see the "airborne dagger" in its physical manifestation but we see it with the "inward eye" (*Daffodils* by *Wordsworth*) and experience the same horror as Macbeth.

Perhaps, as Andy McLean says, the most unsettling feature of this play is that it forces us to enter the imagination of the Macbeths. We become helpless witnesses to the moral degradation of the characters and there is no way one can remain aloof to the tragedy of the couple because of this. The Witches are visible to only Macbeth, Banquo and us. Banquo's ghost shaking its "gory locks" can be seen by only Macbeth and us. When we see Lady Macbeth sleepwalking and crying "Out, out, damned spot!", only we know that she is talking of Duncan's blood. Only we in the audience understand the fragments of past conversations that she is reliving in her unhinged mind. Because of our silent participation in their mental deterioration, we realise the psychology that propels a "formidable warrior and his fiercely intelligent wife towards madness and death." (Andy McLean) Those without imagination will be unable to enjoy the play for it will then be nothing more than a gory spectacle of bloodshed.

Again, the swiftness of the play's action can only be matched by a flight of the imagination. The energy in the quick changes of scene from heath to battlefield to castle in the first part of the play runs parallel to the energy of emotions the Macbeths demonstrate in these scenes. And this energy is transmitted from the page to the stage and then to the audience through the imagination. An empty hall is filled with a hum as the audience seats itself. Silence descends as the curtain lifts. And straightaway we are plunged into the darkness that *Macbeth* epitomises. The writer transmits his imagination to the actors who, in turn, transmit it to the audience. And so we become partners-in-imagination to view how imagination toys with two people and disguising ruin as greatness destroys them completely. *Macbeth* is compelling in the way it draws our imagination which does not give us a moment's respite from the breakneck pace of the play's action.

3. **Presence of Macbeth in Bengali Theatre.**

Shakespeare came to India even before Macaulay, who propagated English education to create a class of educated civil servants to help in administering the British Empire, insisted on its inclusion in the English curriculum. Henry Derozio of the Hindu College, now Presidency University, not only taught Shakespeare but had his students present excerpts from plays such as *Julius Caesar, Macbeth, Cymbeline, Troilus and Cressida* etc. from 1827. Other institutions upholding this tradition were the Oriental Seminary, Metropolitan Academy, St. Xavier's College and David Hare Academy. These amateur presentations were hosted in the private theatres of the affluent Bengalis and catered to a niche audience of an educated class. Calcutta being the capital of the British then, a number of European style playhouses such as The Calcutta, Athenaeum, Chowringhee, and Sans Souci came into existence. Both the actors and audience were whites. The Hindu Theatre opened on December 28, 1831 for performances of exclusively English plays. With time, the Bengali stage acquired enough maturity and independence to not only critique their colonial masters through their dramaturgy but also to assimilate the earlier rejected traditional roots through historical and mythical drama. Although Shakespeare exerted an influence on dramatists like Madhusudan Dutt, Dinabandhu Mitra and Dwijendralal Roy, productions of his plays, translated or adapted versions, began only in 1870.

In 1874, a tutor gave the task of translating Shakespeare's *Macbeth* into Bengali verse to a boy who was at the tender age of thirteen. His Sanskrit tutor showed the verse to the pre-eminent Bengali scholar of the time Pandit Ishwar Chandra Vidyasagar who praised it. The essayist Rajkrishna Mukhopadhyay who was also present with Vidyasagar suggested varying the verse and metre of the witches' scenes from those of the other characters. The boy did as advised and his compositions of the Witches' dialogues (the only extant pieces of this adolescent's translation) were published in the journal *Bharati*. The Bengali reader will have guessed who the boy was – yes, none other than the Bard of Bengal, Rabindranath Tagore!

The very same year Haralal Ray published *Rudrapal Natak*, his translation of the play and it was followed the next year, that is 1875 by Taraknath Mukhopadhyay's *Macbeth*. Ten years later Nagendranath Basu published *Karnabir* followed by Girish Chandra Ghosh's production in 1893 and Ashutosh Ghosh's publication in 1894. One of the reasons for Shakespeare's *Macbeth* being a particular favourite for translation was Bengal's inclination for rebellion against the establishment both before and after independence. With its central conflict revolving around right and wrong governance and the spiritual crisis between desire and conscience, Shakespeare's *Macbeth* provided the Bengali intelligentsia an opportunity to experiment with ideas of violent rebellion against the status-quo, the solitary alienation of despots, and the disastrous consequences of a despotic regime.

The plays are examples of not only translations/adaptations but also transcreations. As their names convey, both *Rudrapal* and *Karnabir* are infused with nationalist sentiment that is predominantly Hindu-oriented. In both, the Norwegian king is referred as 'Jabanraj', from the Sanskrit 'yavana', a trope referring to any foreigner from the West in Hindu literature. The dramatists by the use of this term 'Jaban' remind the Bengali Hindus of the centuries-old persecution and obfuscation of the Hindu cultural heritage and traditions, first by the Muslims and later by the Europeans and ignite their nationalist as well as religious fervour. The foreignness of the play is deliberately erased by the renaming of all major characters – Macbeth is of course Rudrapal and Karnabir, Lady Macbeth is Chaturika and Malina, while the witches are *bhairabis*. The *tantric* cult in Hinduism lends legitimacy to *bhairabis* while even today, witches are devil's followers in Christianity. There is an inclusivity in the translations that could be what Shakespeare had been striving for through his portrayal of the witches as non-binary. Girish Ghosh's *Macbeth* has the honour of being the first of Shakespearean adaptations meant for the commercial stage. It remains faithful to the original for the most part and is often, therefore, criticised as an example of cultural submission to the colonial masters. But his translation is not a mimicry of the English text but an "imaginative and scholarly mediation" of a foreign text in Bengali. Though Girish Ghosh replicated the particulars of the original play, in no way does he prescribe it as a model for emulation. Instead, it reminds us of the tangled weave of collusion and confrontation that is an essential feature of colonial and even modern Bengal.

4. **Shakespeare in Indian Theatre.**

Shakespeare has a pan-Indian appeal and his plays have been performed extensively throughout India for about two hundred years. In fact, to my surprise, I found representations of Shakespeare in the folk and traditional theatre of India. An article from the Hindu News London, April 19, 2016 mentions a survey that acknowledges the better understanding of Shakespeare in India compared to his own country and his fame in the emerging economies of the world far exceeds that in the UK. This is because of the adaptability of his plays. The universality of their themes of revenge, murder, intrigue, separation and reunion, love and betrayal fuse with socio-political situations and the intermix of high rhetoric and low banality make them in tune with the folk traditions of *jatra, nautanki, kathakali* etc.

Shakespeare was introduced to India with the introduction of Westernised education for the grooming of a class of *babus* who would serve in secondary roles in the government administrative offices under the English masters. Theatre houses were built during 1775-1808 in the then capital of India, Calcutta, to entertain the British officers and their *babus*. Plays like *Othello, The Merchant of Venice, Hamlet, Romeo and Juliet, Richard III, Comedy of Errors* and *The Taming of the Shrew* were among the most popular. These plays were translated and adapted around 1850 first into Bengali followed by Marathi, Gujrati, Hindi and Urdu.

It was however the Parsi theatre companies whose presentations took Shakespeare to the populace. The greatest Parsi playwright and producer was Agha Hashr Kashmiri whose versions of *King Lear* (*Safed Khoon*) and *Macbeth* (*Khwab-e-hasti*) were highly successful; his adaptations had powerfully plots with faithful renditions of passion and violence along with musical and comic interludes. In general, to provide an Indianised version of the plays, the companies often deviated from the original text and filled the plays with songs and dances and melodrama to make it more appealing to their un-English audience. This style came to be known as the Parsi style characterised by musical performance styles a la 19th century courtesans contrasted with the *abhinaya* of classified Sanskrit drama, the techniques of folk theatre running parallel to elements seen in the English performances of European touring companies such as Geoffrey Kendall's *Shakespeareana Theatre Company*. The theatre started losing its appeal with the arrival of films and the Parsi theatres turned into movie studios in the 1920s. The flow of Parsi capital went into the talkies and the Bombay film industry was born. What must be noticed however is that the elements of the Parsi style were retained in this new form of entertainment and so Bollywood movies till the late 1980s had elaborate song and dance sequences interspersed with slapstick comedy and melodrama.

In post-colonial India, Shakeapearean adaptations were presented through a fusion of traditional and folk theatre forms such as Jatra, Yakshagana, Nautanki etc. This resulted, on a deeper level than immediately apparent, an intercultural restablishment of harmonious relations between two hitherto conflicted nations. The Bengali adaptation of *Macbeth* directed by Utpal Dutt, was in the Jatra form and according to Rustom Bharucha it was in all probability "closer to the guts of the Elizabethan theatre than most European revivals of Shakespeare's plays in recent years". The actor-director B V Karanth of National School of Drama, produced one of the finest adaptations of *Macbeth* in Hindi entitled '*Barnam Vanam*' using the folk theatre form of Yakshagana which is characterised by a fluid rhythm and a strong dramatic style. Elements of Oriental theatre traditions found in Bali, Indonesia, Cambodia and Japan were also incorporated in the set design, costume and props. Karant interpreted the play as an 'intricate jungle of ambition' that exists in the mind and traps us in its web, making us our own enemies. All together, it was a unique production and perhaps Shakespeare became truly a "dramatist for all time!"

In 2014, Ratan Thiyam directed a Manipuri version of *Macbeth* produced by the Chorus Repertory Theatre Company. Thiyam treats Macbeth as the epitome of the dreadful disease of unlimited desire, greed and violence that has insidiously destroyed humanity in general and India in particular. Set in the backdrop of the 21st century world, his representation of Macbeth is perhaps the most devastatingly horrifying experience in post-colonial theatre of India.